MARK

Other books by the author:

Luke: The Perennial Spirituality
Matthew: Spirituality for the '80s and '90s
The Lay-Centered Church
John Paul II and the Laity
Laity's Mission in the Local Church
Laity: A Bibliography

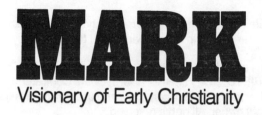

MARK

Visionary of Early Christianity

Leonard Doohan

BEAR & COMPANY
PUBLISHING

SANTA FE, NEW MEXICO

Acknowledgements

I thank my wife Helen for her support throughout the work and especially for her help with the preparation of the index.

Scripture texts used in this work are taken from the NEW AMERICAN BIBLE, COPYRIGHT ©1970, by the Confraternity of Christian Doctrine, Washington, D.C., and used by permission of the copyright owner. All rights reserved.

Part of the chapter on discipleship was first published in No. 58 of Scripture in Church, and I express my gratitude to the editors for permission to use the material in this present work.

Cover Design: William Field, Santa Fe
Photo by Patrice Ceisel
Typography: Copygraphics, Santa Fe
Printed in the United States by BookCrafters, Inc.

For Michael and Frank
"A friend is a friend at all times.
It is for adversity that a friend is born"
(Proverbs 17:17)

Contents

MARK

Introduction
MARK'S CONTEMPORARY CHALLENGE

Mark's is the kind of book that any organization would like to be without! He criticizes the accumulation of inauthentic traditions, portrays the foundation's leaders in poor light, rejects institutional interpretations of theology, and even portrays Jesus in what others consider too human a mold. Within fifteen years of the appearance of Mark's gospel, other evangelists touched up his presentation, left out some of the material that caused frustration and questions, re-established the ecclesiastical right to interpret teaching, and solidly placed Jesus and the Twelve on pedestals of devotion.

Mark is one of the most daring figures of the early Church, but at the same time he is not easily labelled. He is the first to assemble the oral traditions about Jesus, thereby showing his fidelity and devotion to the past. But he is equally forceful in challenging his own Church's accumulated traditions, especially those he does not see as authentically representative of the events of Jesus' life and ministry. He respectfully documents the authority of Church leaders, and still feels free to challenge them. He portrays Jesus as Son of God, but also as angry, impatient, and critical. There are indications that the patristic Church did not quite know how to view him. Each of the four traditional symbols of the evangelists (Rev 4:7) have been applied to Mark: lion by Jerome, calf by Athanasius, human face by Augustine, and flying eagle by Irenaeus.

It is difficult to know what to make of Mark. One point is clear: no Christian of any time can read this gospel without being challenged by it. It is blunt and shocking. Yet Mark's use of characters, his general structure, and his strategical placing of episodes to indicate interpretation show outstanding skill. Mark's gospel may appear simple, but its author is sophisticated both literarily and theologically. If we can resist filling out his text with material from Matthew and Luke, and can concentrate exclusively on what he has to say, he will lead us along one of the most challenging journeys of human history.

Mark's work is "little short of staggering,"[1] and has proved to be "the most enduringly powerful narrative in the history of Western civilization, perhaps in the history of the world."[2] Using the events of Jesus' ministry to form the structure of his gospel, he swiftly draws readers into the events so that they seem to experience them firsthand. His sense of immediacy and urgency affect readers, who soon find they are personally the recipients of this good news.

Return to sources.   Prior to Mark we have the writings of Paul, and oral traditions, but no synthesis or interpretation of the life and ministry of Jesus. Mark selects from many oral traditions those he considers reflect the authentic teachings of or about Jesus. For Mark, "gospel" is both the good news Jesus preached and the good news about him. Mark is the first Christian to put these traditions into writing and thereby stop the influence of disintegrating oral traditions, some of which no longer presented the original events but rather the communities' interpretations of them. Since Mark is the author of the first gospel, he is the filter through which traditions pass; he evaluates their authenticity, and stabilizes the interpretation of faith. He is a man of strong convictions, courage, and prophetical challenge, interested in both the preservation of orthodoxy and creative interpretation that can insure relevancy.

As we examine Mark's work of theological clarification, we will see that he challenges false understandings of messiahship, discipleship, Church, mission, and end times, correcting them by refocusing on the original message of Jesus and its authentic interpretations. In doing so, he confronts those institutions and authorities who ought to be custodians of the message, but in Mark's eyes have failed in their responsibility.

Mark's challenge to his readers to purify traditions and return to sources is as relevant today as in his own time. Today Christian Churches, separated from each other and polarized within, seem incapable of resolving ecumenical differences or uniting their own people. Frequently, we see Christians clinging to the now lifeless traditions of elders rather than returning to the simple call of Jesus that is directed to everyone. In the Catholic tradition, solidified Church structures, the absence of options in ministry, the demeaning treatment of the laity, and reluctance to deal with women's issues all reflect the clutter of traditions, accumulated over centuries of political interaction. Other Christian traditions show similar problems, some of them more extreme than those of Catholicism. All would benefit from Mark's forceful reminder that human traditions, no matter how sacred we think they are, must not block the original authentic message.

A rejection of the comfort zone of religion. Some in Mark's community are seduced by the idea of a great, powerful, miracle-working Christ, who heals, exorcizes, and raises from the dead. Similarly they see their own discipleship as prolonging these manifestations of power. Mark calls them to restudy the original message of the crucified and risen Lord, to realize that there is no Jesus without the cross. Their faith in the suffering Lord is essentially a faith in the cross.

Some of Mark's community, possibly anticipating persecution, needed to understand that their following of Jesus must be motivated, not by hope of miracles (he generally kept these secret), but by willingness to suffer with him. "Mark's Gospel is an invitation to confess in the midst of human tragedy and suffering that Jesus is indeed the Son of Man, the example of how to find life by losing it."[3] There is no easy way to God, like those possibly suggested by the Graeco-Roman world, but only discipleship, faith, and the cross. As Christians journey toward the promised kingdom, they must suffer present trials, thus manifesting their radical faith and hope.

Mark also insists that there are no secure and comforting channels of truth that we can unquestioningly accept. Whether we examine the Temple and its rituals, the Pharisees and their laws, the scribes and their interpretations, or the disciples and their misunderstandings—we find that they all warn us against placing our security in religious institutions of one kind or another. Genuine religion does not guarantee this kind of security.

In today's Christian Churches we see conservatives delighting again in the re-establishment of monarchical power, the rebirth of centralized authority, the dominant influence of career ecclesiastics, the increase in curial trials, the power of wealth, and a return to a fundamentalist interpretation of Church teachings. We also witness a return to the comfort of tridentine mystery, preconciliar devotions, and a facade of security in moral teachings. This yearning for comfort and security, never a sign of authentic religious faith, would be as severely criticized by Mark today, as it was in his own time.

The courage to be free.   While Mark is respectful of sources, authentic teachings, and authorities, he leaves the reader with a sense of profound individual responsibility and liberty. Some in his community, having had to break with the past, are now free of the Temple and pharisaic law; they must not cling to former ways. They are free from the overbearing pressure of Church authorities, that Mark seems to identify with James and the Jerusalem Church. They are free from Satan's hold over them, for Jesus has overthrown and bound him. They are free of their own sin, for Jesus has brought forgiveness. They are free, even though they anticipate persecution and death, for they know that losing one's life for Christ is the way to gain it. In their own religious practice, they are free from the burden of rituals and directives, for the seed of Christian life grows secretly on its own.

Mark portrays a healthy skepticism towards the restrictive dimensions of religion, for Christ has made us free. This freedom brings both joy and responsibility. The constructive role of skepticism and evangelical criticism is needed in all the Churches. While respecting those who minister in management roles, we can never be blind to their failures, their misconceptions and the temptations they experience to seek position and control. Respect for authority is necessary, but we must always be on our guard against its abuse.

In the Churches of the early eighties we see again, as we have so often seen before, Church officials who seek to control others and impose their own views on followers from all walks of life. We see appointments resulting from unquestioning loyalty to other Church administrators rather than to the gospel. We even see ecclesiastical attitudes and curial trials similar to those of which sections of the apocalyptic discourse of Mark are clearly descriptive. Mark's blunt rejection of this type of control and his sense of liberty are challenging and full of hope.

Mark's contemporary challenge.   As we look to the nineties, Christianity continues to be characterized by divisions and polarization. The early enthusiasm of the late sixties has disappeared, and honest attempts at dialogue and coresponsibility have waned. We see a return to the concentration of power and control in the hands of a few. Our division into Churches has extended to divisions within the Churches, and this polarization and hostility seem likely to increase.

We also witness a growing inflexibility in Church structures and the surfacing of an ecclesiastical totalitarianism which is basically a manifestation of weak faith in Christ's presence in all the faithful. These man-made structures should be changed; where they are not changed, they should be confronted.

Many needs of today's Christian people go unmet: the need for respect, freedom, religious experience, dialogue, and sacramental ministers. Much of today's spirituality is inadequate for the modern world, coming from elitist officials, unsure of the Christian challenges in the real world.

These problems in our Churches are not likely to decrease during the next decade, rather they will intensify. The "sorrowful gospel"[4] is very appropriate for our sorrowful Church. Mark's call to suffer, envisioned by him as coming from forces outside the Church, is more likely to come as a result of inner tension, divisiveness, and mutual rejection. Mark's evangelical call to respect authorities, challenge them, and imitate the suffering servanthood of Jesus may indicate the major directions of the next decade's spirituality.

Mark's call to return to authentic sources, uncluttered by unacceptable traditions; his challenge away from the comfort zone of religion; and his insistence on allowing people to live as those freed by the Lord may well be the main trends of the next decade's ecclesial responsibility.

His reminder to break with the past, and to live an independent reincarnation of Jesus' call in the present, selecting from the available traditions those still relevant, may be the focus of our pastoral practice.

Mark is a genius, a prophet, and an irritant, who will always disturb our comfortable, unquestioned lives. A Christian without compromise, his message is one of the most challenging documents of world history.

Chapter One
MARK: THE AUTHOR

*Keep salt in your hearts and you will be at peace
with one another. (Mk 9:50)*

Mark, the author of the second gospel, is the first theologian of
early Christianity to bring order into the many oral traditions about
Jesus. The Lord died around the year 30, and since the early
communities expected his immediate return, they felt no need to
compile a written account of the traditions concerning him. In
the year 50, Paul began to write letters to his communities, but
these seem more like evangelization by correspondence, supply-
ing pastoral answers to local questions, than a detailed and
ordered synthesis of the Lord's ministry and teachings. Mark's is
the first gospel, and although Matthew and Luke stylistically im-
proved Mark's work and made further theological applications;
nevertheless, Mark is the genius who gave us the first written
gospel, having selected and arranged the material to give an insightful interpretation of Jesus' life and ministry.

All the great New Testament writers come after Mark. Before
him there is only oral tradition and Paul's letters. Mark stands
alone as the inventor of the gospel form. This fact itself shows
Mark's genius and creativity, his foresight and vision of an expanded Christianity.

Oral tradition concerning Jesus had circulated for over thirty
years before the appearance of Mark's work. These traditions included not only the words of Jesus, but local Churches' interpretations of Jesus' significance for them. From these traditions,
Mark selects those he considers important for his community.
This very process of selection implies evaluation of the traditions' suitability for the new situations faced by Mark's community. It equally presumes his omission or conscious rejection
of other traditions viewed inappropriate or irrelevant to his community's needs. He is a courageous disciple who focuses the

challenge of Jesus for his community, drawing the Lord's message from the chaos of innumerable oral traditions. Without Mark, Christianity might easily have experienced the same disintegration of its founder's teaching, as have other less fortunate world religions. Fifteen years after Mark completed his gospel, it was still the basis for further interpretations of Jesus' teaching in Matthew and Luke.

Unlike Matthew's gospel, Mark's work did not have immediate major influence throughout the Church. Moreover, for twenty centuries Mark's gospel has been more neglected than any other. Nevertheless, interest in Mark as a theologian and an outstanding dramatic writer began to develop in the 1960s.

Early Traditions and Contemporary Views of Authorship

The unanimous conviction of early historians. The first reference to the authorship of the second gospel comes from Papias, bishop of Hieropolis in Asia Minor, who lived around 60-130. In his *Exegesis of the Lord's Oracles*, a lost work referred to by Eusebius in his *Church History*, Papias quotes an even earlier source, the Elder, as saying: "Mark, having become the interpreter of Peter, wrote down accurately all that he remembered of the things said and done by the Lord, but not however in order." This early statement of the Elder is reaffirmed by Papias,[1] and his conclusions are then accepted by Justin, Irenaeus, Clement of Alexandria, Origen, Tertullian, and Jerome.[2] They are also restated in the anonymous Anti-marcionite Prologue and the Muratorian canon.[3] The unanimous conviction of the early writers is that Mark, the author of the second gospel, is the same Mark as the companion of Peter (1 P 5:13), also referred to in the missionary work of the early Church (Acts 12:12, 25; 13:5-13; 15:36-39; Col 4:10; Phlm 24; 2 Tim 4:11).

These early authorities agree that Mark was "the interpreter of Peter." Irenaeus and the Anti-marcionite prologue add that Mark wrote the second gospel "after the death of Peter." The Muratorian canon further insists that "at some things he was present, and so he recorded them." Clement of Alexandria goes even futher, telling us that Peter knew what Mark was doing, and at first "he neither actively prevented nor encouraged the undertaking," but later he tells us that Peter "ratified the writing for reading in the Churches," so that we can be assured that "the Gospel which is called according to Mark . . . [is compiled from] . . . the things which were spoken by Peter." Tertullian agrees with this last statement. Origen later tells us that in his gospel Mark "did as Peter instructed him." The Anti-marcionite prologue states that Mark wrote his gospel "in the regions of Italy." Clement is more specific, and twice says the work was done in Rome.

The patristic writers presume that the author of the second gospel is "my son Mark," referred to in Peter's first letter (1 P 5:13), and usually identify him with John Mark from the Acts of the Apostles (Acts 12:12, 25).

All the evidence from early writers combines to form a biography of the second evangelist. He is presented as Mark (his Roman name), also called John (his Aramaic name), who lived his early life in Jerusalem, where his mother let their home be used for the gatherings of the early Church (Acts 12:12). Mark, a cousin of Barnabas (Col 4:10), began his missionary work with Paul and Barnabas (Acts 12:25; 13:5). In Pamphylia Mark left the missionaries and returned home (Acts 13:13), a departure Paul viewed as desertion and because of it later rejected Mark for the second missionary journey (Acts 15:38). As a result of this quarrel, Mark joined Barnabas in a mission to Cyprus (Acts 15:39). Later, Paul and Mark having been reconciled, we again find Mark accompanying Paul (Col 4:10), as his colleague (Phlm 24) and useful helper in the work (2 Tim 4:11). After these missionary experiences with Paul and Barnabas, we find Mark with Peter in Rome (1 P 5:13), following his preaching and later becoming his authorized interpreter.

The second gospel contains many indications of the author's association with Peter. The public ministry begins with the call of Peter (1:16-18), Jesus' first miracle is the cure of Peter's mother-in-law (1:30), and Peter is named first among the apostles (3:17). Some sayings that Matthew ascribes to the disciples, Mark explicitly attributes to Peter (11:21). Finally, the young man in white robes expressly refers to Peter in his resurrection mandate (16:7). Futhermore, some episodes such as Jesus' rebuke of Peter (8:33) and Peter's denial of the Lord (14:66-72) are recorded with details typical of eyewitness accounts. Some commentators suggest that Peter's speeches in Acts (Acts 10:34-43) are very similar to the preaching in Mark and believe this confirms Acts as a record of Peter's missionary preaching.

Most modern commentators are impressed with the unanimous testimony of the early writers to the authorship of Mark; as many as seventy-five percent are convinced that the author of the second gospel is Mark, Peter's disciple, and the John Mark of Acts. This position they regard as "virtually certain," "not open to serious doubt," and think it "may be accepted as sound." "There can be no doubt" they state about the evangelist's association with Peter, for it is based on "unbroken testimony," and "is held almost with complete unanimity."[4]

In the second gospel, then, according to the views of the early Fathers of the Church and three out of every four modern commentators,[5] "One man, overwhelmed by a second man's memories of a colossal third man, preserves these memories as an urgent legacy to our race."[6]

Recent questions regarding authorship. The unanimity of early Church writers concerning the authorship of the second gospel is not due to a consensus derived from a variety of different sources, since all of the sources are dependent on Papias, a writer who has rarely generated broad support and confidence either in his own time or in ours. The patristic tradition concerning Mark involves a progressive embellishment of the Elder's comments. From interpreter, Mark becomes attending recorder, who personally initiates the compiling of Peter's sermons. Later, we are told Peter was indifferent, then that he ratified the work, and finally that he was the initiator, instructing Mark to do it. Since all the early witnesses are dependent on Papias, the only independent witness, this testimony of history is weak. The second gospel has little, if any, evidence in support of Mark's association with Peter, so unless Papias had said that Mark was Peter's interpreter probably no one else would have suggested it.

The gospels circulated anonymously until the second century. When names were added, this gospel was ascribed to Mark. While this may well have been his name, it is unnecessary to identify him with the John Mark of Acts or the Mark of Peter's first letter. The early Church required apostolic authorship for the gospels, and the identification of the three Marks was both convenient and assuring. It is, of course, possible that John Mark wrote the second gospel; it is also possible that it was based on a tradition from Peter or done under his patronage. However, there are as many arguments against these positions as there are in support of them.

Examining the detailed portrait of John Mark presented by the New Testament, we find he is quite unlike the author of the second gospel.[7] John Mark is a Jew, whereas the second gospel shows little interest in the Jews and is even critical of them (7:1-23). John Mark is from a wealthy, priestly family in Jerusalem, and travels extensively. The second evangelist, however, seems unfamiliar with Jerusalem, shows no signs of coming from either a priestly or a wealthy family, and seems to be confused about the geography of Palestine. Although John Mark lived in Jerusalem at the time of Jesus and personally knew the Twelve and probably Mary, no one has ever claimed that the second gospel is the work of an eyewitness to Jesus' ministry; it virtually ignores Mary, and portrays the Twelve in bad light. John Mark is principally associated with Paul, and after an initial unfortunate experience, goes on to become a trusted co-worker. Yet, the second gospel shows no Pauline influence.[8]

Patristic tradition also asserts that the second gospel is based on Peter's preaching in Rome. Apart from a reference in the *Shepherd of Hermas*, and possible use in Clement's first letter, the second gospel is soon displaced by Matthew's, an unlikely event were Mark truly of Petrine authority. Augustine refers disdainfully to Mark as "an abbreviator in the footsteps of Matthew."[9] Furthermore, the touches that suggest an eyewitness and the emphasis on episodes involving Peter are adequately accounted for by oral tradition.[10]

The second gospel is not derived directly from the preaching of one man. Many doublets show that Mark had more than one source, and the "material bears all the signs of having been community tradition"[11]—rather than being based solely on the preaching of Peter.

The second evangelist is not likely to be John Mark. Too many difficulties attend this convenient collage of Papias. Rather, our writer is Mark, an anonymous figure from the early Church, whose dedication and genius stemmed the disruptive effects of the disintegration of oral tradition. His work marks the transition from the local apostolate of the first generation to the universal vision of the Gentile Church, and provides the latter with a coherent synthesis of Jesus' message.

The First Gospel Ever Written

The priority of Mark. First century writings offer only two possible references to Mark's gospel, and the first clear use of it comes after 150. By the turn of the century Matthew's was the most extensively used gospel, while Mark's had faded into obscurity. By the last quarter of the second century all four gospels had been universally accepted as canonical. Sometimes they were grouped in the order in which it was thought they were written: Matthew, Mark, Luke, and John; sometimes in an order indicative of their presumed apostolic authorship: Matthew, John, Luke, and Mark. In either case, the inferiority of Mark's text was presumed. Furthermore, it was not until the fifth century that Victor of Antioch wrote the first known commentary on Mark; three centuries later the Venerable Bede wrote his; and in the twelfth century Euthymius Zigabenus, a monk from Constantinople, wrote the third of the ancient commentaries.[12]

This neglect of Mark was due to the conviction that his gospel was an abridgement of Matthew's. The latter was believed to be the work of an apostle, whereas Mark's was not. Matthew's was twice Mark's length, superior as a catechetical aid, and its teachings more attractive to church leaders.[13]

Historical and literary analyses, developed in biblical criticism since the seventeenth and eighteenth centuries, have reversed scholars' estimation of Mark. Few writers today believe Mark is an abbreviation of Matthew. Mark's gospel is simple, vivid, lifelike, enigmatic, and without some of the later theological refinements. Matthew's gospel is a stylistic development of Mark's, using 8,555 of Mark's 11,078 words, reproducing 709 of Mark's 855 sentences, and copying exactly 136 of them.[14] Matthew's gospel portrays a later Church, omits the theologically problematic parts of Mark's, and adds teachings of Jesus that Mark would surely not have omitted had he been dependent on Matthew.

In 1826, G. Wilke presented the first evidence that Matthew used Mark. In 1835, K. Lachmann demonstrated that Matthew and Luke follow the same order only when they both follow Mark. C. H. Weisse in 1838, and H. J. Holtzmann in 1863, both insisted on the priority of Mark. Today the majority of scholars presume this priority, and many have written excellent syntheses of the aims of Matthew and Luke, based on the conviction that they used and modified Mark. Whereas, no acceptable analysis of Mark has been based on the assumption that he abbreviated Matthew.[15]

When Matthew and Luke wrote their gospels they had Mark and Q as sources, but Mark had no written synthesis of the ministry and teachings of Jesus. As the first to write a gospel, Mark must be respected as a daring evangelist who integrated the traditions about Jesus and presented them along with his own creative interpretations and insight.

Mark's sources.   A small number of scholars today still support Matthew's as the first gospel and primary source of Mark's,[16] others propose one common Hebrew or Aramaic source for the synoptics.[17] S. E. Johnson suggests Mark may have used one of several versions of Q.[18] P. Parker postulates "K," a koiné Greek source, as a common source used by Mark and Matthew.[19]

Source analysis is more difficult in Mark's case than in Matthew's and Luke's, since the latter can be compared in their use of Mark or Q, but this process cannot be used for Mark. Some writers focus on what they consider are identifiable oral sources and suggest that the gospel's strong Semitic flavor points to an Aramaic oral tradition, or that its scattered presumed paulinisms indicate connections with the Apostle of the Gentiles, or even propose that "behind the Marcan form of the narrative it is sometimes possible to detect Peter's voice."[20]

Some writers, recognizing the general unity of Mark's presentation, feel that the many episodes of obviously mature oral tradition, together with the many doublets, evidence his use of sources.[21] Possible sources suggested include a sayings collection,[22] a cycle of miracle stories,[23] two traditions (each composed of a feeding, a crossing of the lake, a controversy, and a teaching related to bread),[24] the controversies of chapter two,[25] the parables of chapter four,[26] a collection of Old Testament proof texts combined with traditions about Jesus,[27] a passion narrative,[28] and a possible written source made up of a collection of teachings introduced with "be on your guard."[29]

The best known theory regarding sources of Mark's gospel is the proposal that the text has gone through more than one stage, and at an earlier time consisted of a shorter, relatively simple Palestinian gospel, referred to as the Proto-Mark, or Urmarkus. This earlier gospel, presumed by many to have been the version of Mark used by Matthew and Luke, is thought to have been later expanded into our present form for use in the Gentile world. The main difficulty with this hypothesis is the general unity of our present text of Mark.

Theories as to the sources of Mark's gospel, then, can be grouped as follows: it is an abbreviation of Matthew's; it utilizes sources common to the synoptics; it depends upon the oral teachings of one or another important early Church or Church leader; it utilizes smaller well-formed traditions of various kinds; it depends on a shorter Urmarkus.

Certainly, "no extensive written sources underlie Mark."[30] He draws together many of the oral traditions that had circulated in his Church for about three decades. Some of these were already in relatively fixed oral forms. The above suggestions of commentators give indications as to the possible origin of the oral traditions. Mark, however, without the aid of written sources, integrates these traditions into the first connected written gospel of the Church.[31]

Markan material. The second gospel utilizes oral traditions which Mark collects, stitches together, comments on, and interprets for his community. Simply stated, the material is of two kinds: that which he inherits from the community, and that which he contributes through his editorial work.

The preaching of Jesus was passed on in an exclusively oral form for about fifteen years after the death of the Lord. Paul then began writing letters and continued this practice for twelve to seventeen years. When Mark compiled the second gospel, the oral traditions had already been interacting with each other, been applied to community needs, modified, and reinterpreted over the course of thirty-five years. During this time many of the traditions had gained a fixed form, while others had lost their original context.

The early communities, interested particularly in the teachings of Jesus, circulated the Lord's sayings on issues important to their local Church, often embodying the sayings as the climaxes in short narratives. These *pronouncement stories*, of which there are about twenty in Mark, focus on a dominical saying important to Mark's community.[32]

Jesus undoubtedly presented many of his teachings in *parables*. While each gospel applies them to their own communities, they still "reflect with peculiar clarity the character of his [Jesus'] good news, the eschatological nature of his preaching, the intensity of his summons to repentance."[33] Mark contains six parables, five of which deal with growth.[34]

Among the *sayings of Jesus* are words of wisdom, prophetic or apocalyptic challenges, and legal or ecclesiastical directives. Sometimes without context, they are just strung together with stitchwords, or catchwords that serve as memory aids in catechetical instruction.[35]

As the early communities broke away from Judaism and had to deal with theological conflict, several of the Lord's sayings took on the form of controversy with the Jewish authorities of his own time. Some commentators see a specific source lying behind Mark's *controversies*.[36]

Mark contains twenty-one *miracle stories* that describe the great deeds of the Lord. Achtemeier saw these as forming a pre-Markan source, possibly two parallel miracle cycles: one describing miracles in a Jewish locale, and the other in Gentile regions.[37]

Turning to the editorial contributions of Mark, we find a series of *Markan constructions*: summaries of the mission of Jesus (1:32-34; 3:7-12; 6:12-13, 53-56), and transitional passages that move the reader to the next section (1:22, 28; 2:13; 4:1; 5:1). Sometimes Mark models one episode on the vocabulary and structure of a previous one: the feeding of the four thousand is modeled on the feeding of the five thousand, the cure of the man at Bethsaida on the cure of the deaf mute, the preparation of the passover on the entry into Jerusalem.[38] Taylor points out that sometimes the kernel of a tradition is given, but the narrative is an artificial construction. Seven of the eighteen Markan episodes deal with the Twelve.[39] Although some writers have viewed the passion narrative and the apocalyptic discourse in chapter thirteen as pre-Markan traditions, more likely they are sayings of the Lord and small community traditions molded by Mark into integrated narratives.

Mark's is the first gospel, and although it is independent of major written sources, it draws together traditions, many of which were already well formed for distinct community purposes. However, Mark's own skilful editorial contributions are equally evident.

Mark's Stylistic Characteristics

Mark's style. The author of the second gospel has been referred to as "a man of little culture," "a clumsy writer unworthy of mention in any history of literature,"[40] whose work was judged stylistically crude, artless, weak in theological and literary skill, and lacking the uniform imprint of a genuine author.[41] But in 1978 British actor Alec McCowen recited Mark on the London and New York stages. Audiences and critics welcomed the recitation as an enthralling performance, not to be missed, and McCowen claimed that Mark's gospel was the greatest script he had ever found.[42]

Mark's language is not the elegant Greek of Luke, but rather the simple colloquial Greek used in everyday life. He uses 1270 separate words, more Latinized words than any other New Testament writer, and his Greek presentation still retains the flavor of Palestine, even though he consistently translates Aramaic words (3:17; 5:41; 7:11, 34; 10:46; 14:36; 15:22, 34). What Mark lacks in vocabulary and refinement, he makes up for in a strikingly fresh presentation, filled with vivid details. His work contains only two discourses (4:2-34; 13:5-36), and generally focuses on the events of Jesus' ministry, which he describes with such concrete detail that "each pericope presents a slice of real life."[43] Mark's gospel is so lifelike some commentators unnecessarily conclude it is a primitive narrative, and based on eyewitness accounts.

This literary skill of Mark enables him to focus the reader's attention on the thrilling stories he describes. Conversation and discourse take second place to vigorous and exciting accounts of Jesus' actions. Moreover, Mark creates a sense of urgency in his recounting of Jesus' ministry by the frequent use of "and" or "immediately," a simple technique that "lends a sense of vividness and excitement to the action."[44] He further emphasizes a sense of urgency by reducing references to time and place and by portraying Jesus as moving frequently and hurriedly from one place of ministry to another. This sense of urgency, together with a skilful use of rhetorical questions (4:41), draws the reader into a quickly moving drama, and serves "to make Jesus the contemporary of those who hear or read the account."[45]

Admittedly, Mark is not always clear and exciting, but which author is? In addition to lacking precision in geographical and chronological detail, some stories are only loosely tied together

with stereotyped formulas (9:48-50; 11:22-25), and connections
or development are not evident (2:1-3:6). At times Mark
digresses by giving distracting details (5:1-20, 25-34). His expressions are poor in places: he uses the same phrase to express more
than one meaning (3:5, 34; 5:32; 10:21, 27); his repetitions are
frequently redundant (1:42; 8:17; 13:19, 20); some stories lack his
usual artistic touch and are clearly well-worn traditions, inserted
with little literary effort (2:18-20, 23-28; 3:31-35); and in some
places entire stories are modeled on previous ones (4:39-41 and
1:25-27; 8:22-26 and 7:32-36; 11:1-6 and 14:13-16).

In spite of the above weaknesses, Mark is an outstanding
author; his work, a narrative masterpiece. He masters the traditions, arranges them cohesively, and presents them so appealingly
that he draws the readers into the story.

Literary techniques used by Mark. Mark rarely comments on
the material or extensively editorializes the traditions; rather he
shows his skill in the way he conveys teachings through the
strategic arrangement of the material he selects. Mark's stories
portray concrete episodes from the life of Jesus. He has edited
the material only slightly, if at all, preferring to let it speak for
itself. As a result, the words of Jesus and the accompanying narratives retain much of the atmosphere of Palestine, enabling
readers to appreciate "the conditions which obtained in the oral
period and to learn much about the life of the primitive Christian
communities."[46] This Palestinian atmosphere is also evident in
Mark's frequent quotations from the Septuagint Bible—sixty-
three in all. Only Jesus and the authorities quote the Bible, but
some of the references are not from individual prophets, but syn-
thetic quotations, combined by Mark to more appropriately present his theological understanding of the episodes described.[47]

Mark's desire to let traditions speak for themselves leads him
at times to repeat episodes, including doublets found in the traditions, without choosing between them or synthesizing them into
a single presentation. At times he deliberately uses the same
words or phrases in the course of a narrative, thereby stressing
the issue of interest: forgiveness of sin (2:5, 7, 9, 10), Jesus'
acceptance of sinners (2:15, 16, 17), or the return to the desert
(6:31, 32, 35). Repetition is carried a step further in Mark's
preference for threes: three commissioning stories (1:16-20;
3:13-19; 6:7-13,30), three predictions of passion and resurrection

(8:31; 9:31; 10:33-34), three scenes of Jesus at prayer (1:35; 6:46; 14:32-42), and three episodes on the mountain (3:13; 6:46; 9:2).

Mark also stresses episodes with a more subtle form of repetition, a two-step progression in which he either foreshadows the episode before presenting it, or having presented it, looks back in retrospect. Prophecy, the simplest form of foreshadowing, is frequently used, especially when Jesus foretells his own or his disciples' fate. The reader is thus led to anticipate an event which is later narrated. Rhoads and Michie conclude: "The two-step progression is the most pervasive stylistic feature in the gospel. It occurs in phrases, sentences, pairs of sentences, and the structure of episodes."[48] This two-step progression is an interpretative technique, whether used in sentences, episodes, or the two parts of the gospel.

Parallelism is typical of Semitic composition, and signs of it are identifiable in the material used by Mark, notably contrast parallelism: Peter's misunderstanding of Jesus is contrasted with Jesus' correct understanding of his mission (8:29-32); Peter's superficial rebuke of Jesus is contrasted with Jesus' justifiable condemnation of Peter (8:32-33); Peter's human way of thinking is contrasted with Jesus' divine way (8:33).

A more detailed form of parallelism is inverted parallelism, or chiasm, in which episodes are arranged in a concentric relationship (ABCDC'B'A'). Examples are the arrangement of the five controversies (2:1-3:6) and the debate about the sources of Jesus' power (3:20-35).[49]

A technique used by Mark more than by any other New Testament writer is the insertion of material as a unit in the middle of another unit. Some commentators, focusing on the inserted unit, speak of this technique as inclusion, or interpolation. Others, emphasizing the two parts of the main unit, refer to this technique as framing, or bracketing. This device heightens the dramatic impact of the narrative and also provides commentary on the material. Both the outer bracketing material and the inner unit illuminate each other; more specifically, some commentators feel it is the inner unit that focuses the interpretation to be given to the larger framing material. Thus, the healing and illumination of the disciples is framed by the healing of two blind men (8:22-10:52); the two stages of the story about Jarius' daughter frame the faith of the woman with a hemorrhage (5:21-43); and the two parts of Peter's denial frame the Lord's trial (14:53-72).

One of the less exciting features of Mark, already mentioned, is his use of summaries—highly stylized, clearly editorial statements that synthesize what has gone before or anticipate what is to come (1:14-15; 3:7-12; 4:33-34; 6:53-56). These Markan constructions force the reader to pause and focus on the implications of the narrative before moving to the next section.

Mark is skilful in involving the reader in the drama he describes. Recent literary critics have emphasized the influence of dramatic art forms contemporary with Mark's gospel on its literary character.[50] Readers of the second gospel are placed in the role of the director, or narrator of a drama. This involves the reader, who already knows how everything will turn out, and can therefore appreciate the paradox of Jesus being mocked as a false prophet at the very time his prophecy concerning Peter is being fulfilled (14:65, 72), or the irony of Jesus' being referred to as a king by disbelievers (15:2, 32). Mark's use of rhetorical questions leads readers, who already know the answers, to affirm their belief in Jesus (8:27), to use their imagination regarding their own possible failures (8:33; 9:19), and to realize that even those most dedicated can still apostasize (14:50).[51]

When Mark wrote, he did not know our modern methods of outlining or subdividing a work. He had to rely on the literary techniques of his own cultural milieu. Nevertheless, he combines the oral traditions with a literary skill and insight that give them new life and make them challenge his own community—and for that matter, ours too.

Studies of Mark's Gospel

Mark the compiler: from early times to form criticism. We can learn a lot about the author of the second gospel from tradition, from the realization that he was the first to compile a gospel, and from an examination of the sources and stylistic techniques he used. But we can also gain insight into Mark from the emphases of scholars in the course of two thousand years.

Up to the nineteenth-century Mark was viewed as an abridgement of Matthew and not worthy of separate analysis. Overshadowed by Matthew, Mark was practically ignored. Early Fathers echoed Papias' claim that Mark was the secretary to Peter, and added a little biographical information, but actually not until Jerome did anyone comment on Mark. After Jerome's ten homilies, we must wait until the late fifth century for the first complete commentary, that of Victor of Antioch.[52]

Many reflections or sermons and four complete commentaries on Mark are included in the work of medieval scholars. The reformers' return to the Bible in the sixteenth century stimulated ways of interpretation, but produced few commentaries on Mark as an independent gospel.

Critical approaches to the New Testament started with the works of R. Simon (1689) and H. S. Reimarus (1694-1768). The latter began a period of liberal analysis of the gospels and became the catalyst for biblical critical studies. J. W. Griesbach also deserves mention, since he proposed that Mark was the third gospel written, and depended on both Matthew and Luke, a position that reappears today in modified forms.

Nineteenth-century commentators had two great interests: source criticism and the search for the historical Jesus. The work of source critics such as C. G. Wilke, K. Lachmann, C. H. Weisse, and H. J. Holtzmann convinced them that Mark was the first gospel written, while theologians such as D. F. Strauss, A. Jülicher, and M. Kähler concluded that the most primitive portrait of Jesus was that by Mark.

For eighteen centuries Mark has been bypassed as a rather crude abridgement of Matthew. Critical analysis of the Bible began in the late seventeenth to early eighteenth centuries, and by the end of the nineteenth century a general consensus had been reached that Mark was not an abridgement, but the earliest gospel.

Twentieth-century form critics accepted the priority of Mark, but insisted that his gospel was a compilation of many independent units of tradition which he had stitched together. Each of these units, or forms, had its own history in the early Church, a history that could be traced in the vocabulary or concepts used and the general form of the stories. K. L. Schmidt was the first to concentrate on the Markan connecting phrases and summarizing or transitional passages, but it is the better-known form critics, M. Dibelius and R. Bultmann, who have had a determinative influence on the studies of Mark.[53] Form critics see the gospel as a literary composition produced from fixed traditions which had circulated in the community for over thirty years. The present form is artificially designed by Mark to reflect the faith of the primitive Church. Although the search for the historical Jesus emphasized the primitive character of Mark, form critics stress that the gospel is not a reliable life of the historical Jesus, but rather a synthesis of early Church belief.

Mark the theologian: redactional studies. The work of later form criticism merges into redaction criticism. The former studies the tradition-history of the independent units that make up the gospel; whereas, the latter studies the ways in which a writer arranges, orders, and connects the material, and readily concludes that by means of these compositional or editorial contributions a writer can emphasize his own theological interpretation of the events described.

S. G. F. Brandon, in *The Fall of Jerusalem and the Christian Church* (1951), suggests that Mark arranges his material after the fall of Jerusalem to establish Christian independence from Judaism and thus avoid the disfavor of the Romans and maintain for Christians a positive relationship with Rome.

P. Carrington in *The Primitive Christian Calendar* (1952) proposes that Mark arranges his material to follow a scheme of liturgical readings and offer lessons for the Christian liturgical year.

The more scholars study Mark's compositional contributions, the more they are impressed by the unity of his work. Rather than emphasizing the independence of the traditions, they concentrate on Mark's theological emphases, maintained precisely by the creative way he shapes the tradition. W. Wrede, as early as 1901, in *The Messianic Secret in the Gospels*, had already stated that Mark's gospel was a profound theological synthesis. However, it is W. Marxsen, a disciple of Bultmann, in his *Mark the Evangelist: Studies on the Redaction History of the Gospel* (1956), who is acknowleged as the leader in a new approach to Mark.

Marxsen sees Mark as a theologian and the second gospel as a unified creative composition: "one sermon" made up of "material from the tradition [that] is reworked and adjusted to the concrete present situation." The work is "composed backward," and "the Risen Lord is speaking."[54] Marxsen proposes that Mark also uses geography and chronology with theological intent. The second gospel is kerygmatic—an exhortation to the early Christians to leave Jerusalem and go to Galilee to await the return of the Lord.

Marxsen is a redaction critic: he studies the editorial contributions of Mark to identify his theological biases.[55] This is more difficult in Mark's case, where only certain forms of critical analysis can be used. In fact, Mark is the test case for redaction criticism. Marxsen's approach has had determinative influence on the study of Mark for a quarter of a century.[56]

Some redaction critics emphasize Mark's christology: J. Screiber (1961) sees Mark as dependent on Paul and as emphasizing christological themes in his editing; C. E. B. Cranfield (1962) sees the gospel as a synthesis of the early Church's faith in Christ; P. Vielhauer (1964) suggests the gospel is structured to emphasize Mark's christology; E. Best (1965) stresses the soteriology of Mark; E. Schweizer (1967) proposes Mark is an attempt to correct inadequate views of Jesus; and G. Minette de Tillesse (1968) refocuses attention on the messianic secret in Mark. More recently, A. P. Martin (1972) suggests that Mark's christology is the basis for his presentation of Christian discipleship; J. R. Donahue (1973) sees the trial scene as structured to emphasize Mark's christological concerns; and J. P. Kealy (1977) sees Mark's as a pastoral christology that challenges the disciples to recommit themselves to the Lord.

Some redaction critics conclude that Mark's focus is ecclesiological and pastoral. E. Trocmé (1963) sees Mark as the product of a breakaway missionary group in the early Church; J. Bowman (1965) suggests Mark is written for a Christian Passover celebration. T. J. Weeden (1968) emphasizes the polemical nature of the gospel, written to attack a false christology held by those who were pillars of the established Church; K. G. Reploh and Q. Quesnell (1969) stress the catechetical value of Mark's work for the community; W. H. Kelber (1974) views Mark as a polemic denouncing the false eschatological hopes of the Jerusalem Church and strongly affirming the importance of the Gentile mission; H. C. Kee (1977) sees Mark as challenging a community awaiting the end of the age.[57]

Mark the dramatist: literary criticism.   Redaction critics focus on the compositional contributions of Mark: his choice and arrangement of material, his vocabulary, style, and strategy, and the general structure he gives the work. The last interest has moved us away from an exclusive focus on the author's use or modification of traditions and led us to an appreciation of the overall structure of his work. Wrede had stressed Mark's creativity, and Marxsen gave insight into the authorial skill of Mark. But now the scholarly approach to Mark is no longer analytical but rather evaluates the "full range of the Evangelist's literary activity," including "concern for the text of the gospel as a totality,"[58] while savoring "the language and literary power of the text itself."[59] This recent work on Mark has developed primarily in North America and is referred to as literary criticism. This critical approach to the gospel builds on the insights of redaction criticism, but also focuses on the way individual passages function in the gospel as a whole, the way motifs and themes characterize the general tone of the presentation, the evangelist's use of his characters in the gospel drama, the gospel's various levels of development, and the writer's use of structural features such as summaries and transitions to give direction to the work. As early as 1976, Norman Perrin concluded: "The interpretation of the Gospel of Mark today requires a sophisticated, eclectic method of approach that can perhaps best be called literary criticism."[60]

Literary criticism is a welcome development, responding to scholars' dissatisfaction with the restrictive conclusions of form and redaction criticism. While the latter are still good prerequisites, emerging models of biblical theology today focus more on seeing how the text speaks to the reader, what general literary impressions it conveys, and what response it generates.[61]

Beginning in 1978, McCowen's recital of Mark's gospel on the stages of the world drew attention to what a good story Mark presents: an exciting combination of drama, tragedy, and humor; a breathtaking account of courage, prophetical challenge, and selfless dedication.

Perrin (1974), skilled as a redaction critic, was a leader on the North American scene in integrating redactional critical skills with general literary criticism. Perrin's expertise as a critic leads him to appreciate that Mark has taken the "daring and imaginative step of telling the story of Jesus' ministry in such a way that the concerns of the risen Jesus for Mark's present Church are in the forefront."[62]

D. Rhoads and D. Michie (1982) clasify Mark as story, and identify his use of the typical techniques of storytelling, distinguishing between what the story is and how it is told. Mark tells the story in the way he does in order "to achieve certain effects upon the reader."[63]

A. Stock (1982) also stresses the importance of studying Mark at a literary level. He sees Mark as modeled on the form of a

Hellenistic drama that draws the audience into the dramatic experience, enabling it to participate in the tragedy and share the feelings of its principal characters. Stock points out that his work is not a new way of interpreting Mark, and claims that some authors have consistently seen Mark as drama.[64]

Contemporary approaches to Mark stress less what the text means in itself, and more how it affects the reader when viewed as an exciting story or dramatic production. This reader-response criticism emphasizes the reader's interaction with the text which is not "a subjective fabrication of the reader, for the text itself guides the reader in its realization."[65]

Mark has thus moved from being ignored to being used to solve the Synoptic problem, or to contribute to the search for the historical Jesus. He now occupies a position of respect from which his spiritual power and challenge is proclaimed again with vigor and vitality, and received with enthusiasm and faith.

Early traditions were unanimous in identifying the author of the second gospel with Mark, the disciple of Peter and a well-known figure of the early Church. This position is not as solidly based as previously presumed. In any case, the greatness of Mark does not consist in his relationship with Peter or with the early Jerusalem Church, but in the success of his gospel, the fruit of his dedicated service to the Church. His was the first gospel ever written, a work of vision and a faithful interpretation of Jesus that would exercise as great an influence as any other writing on the future development of Christianity.

Mark acts as a filter, sifting traditions and deciding which are relevant enough to pass on. As a man of courageous determination, he gives direction to the nascent Church, a direction that Matthew and Luke follow.

His style and purpose, left in the shadows for centuries, come to the fore today, and his gospel is valued by our own culture and modern life as highly as it was when he first proclaimed it. Modern scholars may regret the years of neglect, but disciples in these times of uncertainty can identify with Mark's challenge and appreciate him as one of the greatest visionaries of early Christianity.

Chapter Two
THE WORLD OF MARKAN CHRISTIANITY

*Go now and tell his disciples and Peter, "He is going
ahead of you to Galilee, where you will see him just
as he told you." (Mk 16:7)*

Mark was the first writer to arrange the proclamation of Jesus in
an ordered account following his ministry from baptism by John
to crucifixion. In doing so, the places of Palestine in which Jesus
lived and worked took on special significance for Christians
throughout the empire who otherwise would not have had reason
for any interest. Some of these places were simply referred to by
Mark in his account, but others were used with added symbolic
and theological intent. Mark wrote for Christians who were part
of the expanding Roman empire with its military triumphs, moral
failures, cultural enrichment, and religious persecution. In telling us about Jesus, Mark describes the times in which he lived
but saw those times as part of God's plan, and thus gives us not
chronology but salvation history.

In this second chapter, we will examine Mark's world, based
on Jesus' ministry in Palestine, enriched by his use of geography
for symbolic and theological reasons. We will review the history
and life of the Roman empire and synthesize Mark's theology of
history.

The Ministry of Jesus

Mark's outline of Jesus' ministry. Mark's gospel is structured
in inverted parallelism: wilderness-Galilean ministry-journey to
Jerusalem-Jerusalem ministry-tomb (note: see chapter three).
This structure centers on the journey to Jerusalem, the way of
suffering, and the seams between each of the five sections are
Markan transitional passages. Many signs indicate that the outline
of the ministry is artificially arranged by Mark. John the Baptist

begins the account by announcing the coming of Jesus, and later
the messenger at the tomb ends the account by doing the same
(1:2; 16:5-7). The Galilean ministry contains one discourse
(4:1-34), as does the Jerusalem ministry (13:1-37). Also five controversies occur in each ministry (2:1-3:6; and 11:27-12:37). Six
boat trips take place during the northern ministry (4:35-8:21)
and six references to "the way" during the journey (8:22-10:52).
Chapter 6:31-7:37 parallels the sixfold presentation of 8:1-30, the
former cycle of events focuses on the Jews, the latter on the Gentiles. While other examples could be added, these are sufficient
to show the artificial framework of Mark's account of Jesus'
ministry. The structure is designed to move the reader from the
initial proclamation of Jesus as Christ and Son of God to Peter's
acknowledgement of the former (8:29) and the Gentile centurion's acclaim of the latter (15:39). However, this glory of Jesus
is attained through suffering, as Mark meticulously reemphasizes
at the end of each section of his account by editorially looking
ahead to the passion, referring to plots and wicked designs,
distress and suffering, and a willingness to give up everything
(3:6; 6:6; 8:21; 10:45; 12:44).

Mark sees Jesus' teaching more in the concrete events of
ministry than in sermons. The ministry outline is artificial, and
while based on actual events of Jesus' life, we do not know how
accurately Mark has retold the details of Jesus' ministry, for his
concern is evidently that of a theologian not a chronicler. The
Markan Jesus in his healings and exorcisms reconciles people to
God. In his debates and controversies he demonstrates the inade-
quacy of Judaism and its leaders. By gathering another twelve he
demonstrates his conviction that there is now another covenant.
In the symbolic gestures and words of his ministry, Jesus reveals
the judgement of God against Israel.

Mark is the first to utilize a connecting narrative of the great
deeds of Jesus as his tool to convey his theological convictions. Thus
the outline of the ministry becomes theologically significant.

The Galilean ministry.   The gospel begins by describing
preparatory events in the wilderness. John the Baptist, the
forerunner, announces the powerful one who will come and also
anticipates his death. Jesus, after his own baptism and ritual
designation by the voice from heaven, goes off to the desert
where in imitation of his people's history, he is tested for forty

days (1:12-13). After this period of preparation and John's arrest Jesus begins his own ministry and is probably unknown to the crowds before his appearance in Galilee (6:14). Mark's transitional passage (1:14-15) links Jesus to John's preaching and sets the scene for what lies ahead: a ministry of calling to reform and proclaiming the arrival of the kingdom.

Jesus experiences early acceptance, his teaching is received with astonishment "because he taught with authority, and not like the scribes" (1:22), and his healings amazed the people who "gave praise to God, saying, 'We have never seen anything like this!' " (2:12). This early phase of ministry, one of constant movement from place to place, shows Jesus in great demand: the whole town gathered outside his residence (1:33), everybody is looking for him (1:37), and Jesus can not go about openly (1:45), for people kept coming to him in crowds (2:13).

This early enthusiastic acceptance quickly gives rise to Jesus' controversies with the scribes and Pharisees (2:1-3:35), even though the crowds continue to follow him (3:7), and their numbers are expanded with other interested listeners from Gentile regions (3:8). In view of such success, Jesus summons Twelve from among his disciples "as his companions whom he would send to preach the good news" (3:14).

In chapter four, Mark presents his only recorded Galilean discourse of Jesus: the parable discourse (4:1-34). The large-scale enthusiasm of the earlier chapters now gives way to distinctions between insiders and outsiders, the former will understand the parables, but the latter will not (4:11-12).

Jesus continues his ministry around the Sea of Galilee, in both Jewish and Gentile areas. He demonstrates his power over the elements of nature, evil spirits, sickness, and death. However, this power no longer persuades everyone regarding Jesus' messiahship; some accept him (5:42; 7:37), but others do not (6:1-6). Two parallel cycles follow consisting of a feeding, a crossing of the sea, conflict with the Pharisees, a teaching on bread, and a healing (6:31-7:37; and 8:1-26). The healing of the blind man at Bethsaida plays a significant role, serving both as an ending for the Galilean ministry and as a transition to the journey narrative. It will be complemented by the healing of blind Bartimaeus (10:46-52), the concluding episode in the journey section.

The journey to Jerusalem.   In this center section, Jesus'
ministry is directed to the disciples, enlightening them regarding
the nature of the way of the cross. He focuses on his small group
of followers, instructing them in his need to suffer (8:31; 9:30-32;
10:32-34) and their need to imitate his suffering servanthood
(8:34-38; 9:33-37; 10:35-45).

As Joshua led the people to the land of promise (Numbers
27:18), so Jesus journeys with the new chosen people to the
fulfillment of the Lord's promises. This short section is a reliving
of the nation's historical search for freedom and salvation. Jesus,
bringing to completion Moses' leadership, also ascends the mountain to receive God's revealing word: "This is my Son, my beloved,
Listen to him" (9:7).

The journey narrative is the hinge of the entire Markan enter-
prise. During it Jesus reveals his identity and the nature of his
messiahship—Elijah has come, the times are fulfilled, this is the
Son. However, Jesus immediately redirects the disciples' attention: "Yet why does Scripture say of the Son of Man that he must
suffer much and be despised?" (9:12). Peter recognized the
former (8:29) but must also accept the latter (8:31-33). During
the journey, Jesus gives the disciples teachings against ambition
(9:33-37), envy (9:38-42), scandal (9:43-50), and indignation
(10:35-40). He calls them to put into perspective the values of
marriage (10:2-12), children (10:13-16), wealth (10:17-27), and
rewards (10:28-31).

The disciples "way," like Jesus', is one of facing frustration,
opposition, sacrifice, and suffering, appreciating that this is the
way to God. After the lines are drawn between insiders and outsiders in the Galilean ministry, the journey becomes a rapid
movement to the climactic experience of Jerusalem.

The central section ends with the transitional account of the
healing of blind Bartimaeus. Unlike the first healing (8:22-26),
this one is immediate because of Bartimaeus' faith and results in
his total commitment to a discipleship that includes accompanying Jesus on his journey to Jerusalem (10:52).

Ministry in Jerusalem.   Jesus' ministry in Galilee and during
the journey moves quickly as events "immediately" follow one
another. Once in Jerusalem the pace slows down to a detailed
description of Jesus' ministry. Although this could have lasted up
to six months, Mark compresses it into one week, stressing first

Jesus' unimpeded ministry for three days, each one ending in the temple (11:1-11, 12-19, 20-12:44), and then climaxing his account with the days of trial, passion, death, and resurrection.

From Bethphage, Bethany, and the Mount of Olives, Jesus triumphantly enters the city of Jerusalem and is welcomed by the crowds. Scriptural allusions indicate that this solemn entry is intended as a public messianic demonstration—"a colt on which no one has ridden" (11:2; see Numbers 19:2; Deuteronomy 21:3; 1 Samuel 6:7), the greeting "Hosanna!" and reference to "the reign of our father David" (11:10). However, Mark's presentation is low-key in comparison with Matthew's and Luke's (Mt 21:1-17; Lk 19:28-46). Mark's "Hosanna" could be a simple greeting and little more. Moreover, in Mark, Jesus' entry causes no disturbance, and attracts no attention from the authorities, and since "it was already late in the afternoon" (11:11), and there was little to do, Jesus immediately went back to Bethany. This is very different from Matthew's acclaim of the "Son of David" (Mt 21:9) and Luke's crowds who cry "Blessed be he who comes as king . Peace. . . glory" (Lk 19:38). Moreover, both Matthew and Luke conclude the entrance with the cleansing of the temple, which Mark delays until the next day.

Jesus' second day in Jerusalem includes the cursing of the fig tree and the cleansing of the temple; the former symbolically portraying the fate of the temple.

The third day again ends in the temple, where Jesus debates with the leaders of Judaism. The chief priests, scribes, and elders question his authority (11:27-33), Pharisees and Herodians try to trick Jesus regarding the appropriateness of paying taxes to the Romans (12:13-17), Sadducees assail him with queries on the resurrection (12:18-27), and the scribes question him on the central command of the Law (12:28-34). Jesus not only handles the questioning well, but also asks his own questions (12:35-37), challenges their religious leadership (12:1-12), warns his disciples against the hypocrisy of the scribes (12:38-40), and singles out the poor widow as an example of authentic religious practice (12:41-44). He then leaves the temple and goes to the Mount of Olives, a simple move but reminiscent of Ezekiel's vision of the Shekinah, or presence of God, abandoning the temple (Ezekiel 9:3; 10:18; 10:23).

Seated on the Mount of Olives, looking toward the city, Jesus gives his only discourse in this period of ministry, the longest

uninterrupted instruction in Mark. This apocalyptic discourse is
Jesus' farewell address in which he warns his disciples about the
calamities ahead, describes the scene of cosmic tribulation,
alerts them to false Christs and false prophets, reminds them that
the final act of the cosmic drama will be the return of the Son of
Man, and urges them to be constantly watchful.

The three days of ministry concluded, Mark moves to a detailed
description of the events leading upto the passion: plot, anointing, betrayal, passover, denial, agony, arrest, and trial. Jesus'
final hours of suffering and death are described briefly, without
dwelling on the physical pain. His death brings about the end of
the sanctuary and is appreciated by a single Gentile centurion
(15:39). The epilogue on burial again directs the disciples' attention away from Jerusalem and leaves the reader anxiously
wondering what will happen next.

A Holy Land

Jesus' life and ministry took place in Palestine, a country that
became a holy land for Christians. The following maps give
Palestine's location in the Roman empire (MAP 1), its geography
(MAP 2), and governmental and political divisions (MAP 3), a fur-
ther map shows the important places mentioned in Mark's gospel
(MAP 4), a final map indicates the location of important places in
and around Jerusalem, especially those connected with the
Lord's passion (MAP 5).

Mark's Use of Geography

In many cases, the units of oral tradition that Mark molded into the first written gospel had no specific geography or chronology
associated with them. He provided the details, and in doing so,
was able to use the geography to further his theological emphases.
Traditional Jewish understandings accompany Mark's use of
lake, mountain, and wilderness, to which he added strategic
emphases of his own. While tension had frequently existed between Galilee and Jerusalem, Mark develops this into a theological
tension. In general, geography is used structurally by Mark, as he
describes episodes in carefully selected locations. Desert, sea,
and mountain are each a place of call when first mentioned (1:1-13,
16; 3:13); likewise, they are all places of withdrawal for solitude

and reflection, but as the gospel progresses, they take on rich theological connotations. Galilee is the place of salvation and acceptance, Jerusalem of condemnation and rejection.

Wilderness. The remote, empty, and barren desert is a place of danger, hardship, fear, loss of direction, suffering, and death. It immediately suggests chaos, unfruitfulness, wild animals, and evil spirits. But it is frequently a place of refuge, simplicity of life, test, judgment, and encounter with God. In Israel's history it was a place of danger, rebellion, and sinfulness, but also of revelation, election, covenant, Law, and the birth of a nation. Israel's exodus and desert wanderings became symbolic of the struggle-filled journey to encounter God and the promises. Above all, it evoked the original love, choice, and protection that Yahweh gave to the chosen child, and prophets frequently called the people back to the religious fervor of their origins in the wilderness.[1]

Mark's gospel begins in the wilderness (1:1-13) where John the Baptist, a man of the desert (Isaiah 40:3; 2 Kings 1:8), calls people to the desert to repent in anticipation of the coming of a greater one (1:3-4). Beginning with the prologue, Mark builds on traditional religious symbolism of the desert and develops it into a rich concept: a battleground, place of renewal, refreshment, and recommitment to the ways of God. Although almost every chapter has some reference to wilderness, it is stressed particularly during the Galilean ministry.[2]

In the prologue, the wilderness is the place of repentance in anticipation of the coming of God (1:1-8), of the loving election of the chosen child of God (1:10-11), and of the testing by and confrontation with Satan (1:12-13).

In his ministry, Jesus uses the desert as a place of refuge and prayer (1:35, 45); he also uses it as a meeting place (1:45). Drawn there by the power of Jesus' teachings and miracles, the desert reminds them of their call, and Jesus of his own submission to his Father. After the strenuous work of ministry, Jesus withdraws to the wilderness for prayer (1:35-39; 6:45-46), takes his disciples there for rest and the renewal of their commitment to a desert spirituality (6:31-32).[3] When he is transfigured (9:2-8) his messiahship is affirmed by two men of the desert: Moses and Elijah.

Both feeding stories (6:34-44; 8:1-9) occur in deserted places; signs of God's continued providential care as in the nation's

The Roman Empire at the Death of Octavian

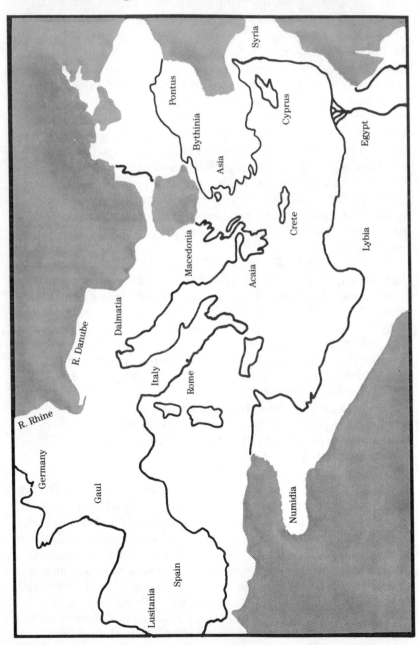

Geography of Palestine

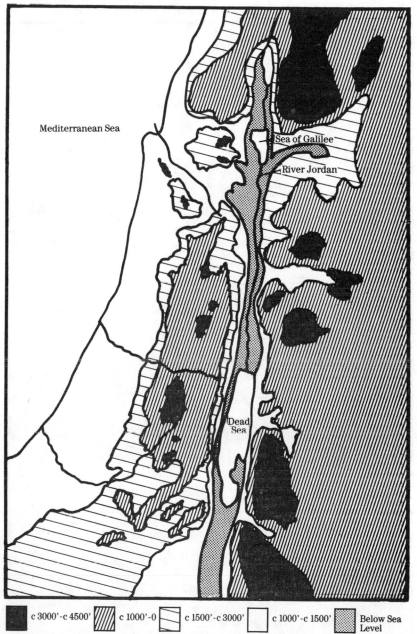

Mediterranean Sea

Sea of Galilee

River Jordan

Dead Sea

c 3000'-c 4500'　　c 1000'-0　　c 1500'-c 3000'　　c 1000'-c 1500'　　Below Sea Level

Government of Palestine During Jesus' Life

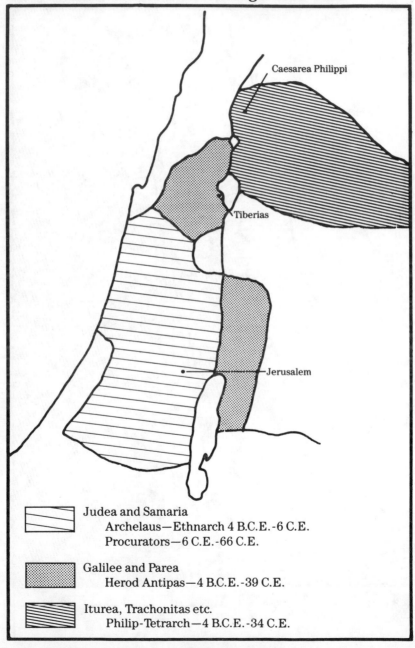

Caesarea Philippi

Tiberias

Jerusalem

Judea and Samaria
  Archelaus—Ethnarch 4 B.C.E.-6 C.E.
  Procurators—6 C.E.-66 C.E.

Galilee and Parea
  Herod Antipas—4 B.C.E.-39 C.E.

Iturea, Trachonitas etc.
  Philip-Tetrarch—4 B.C.E.-34 C.E.

Places mentioned in Mark's Gospel

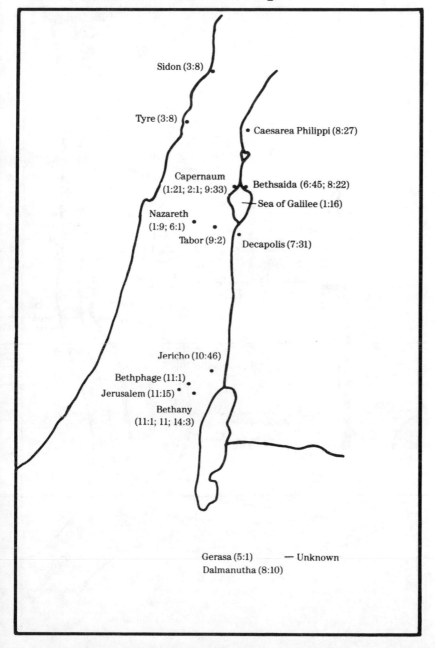

Sidon (3:8)

Tyre (3:8)

Caesarea Philippi (8:27)

Capernaum
(1:21; 2:1; 9:33)

Bethsaida (6:45; 8:22)

Sea of Galilee (1:16)

Nazareth
(1:9; 6:1)

Tabor (9:2)

Decapolis (7:31)

Jericho (10:46)

Bethphage (11:1)

Jerusalem (11:15)

Bethany
(11:1; 11; 14:3)

Gerasa (5:1)   — Unknown
Dalmanutha (8:10)

Jerusalem in the New Testament

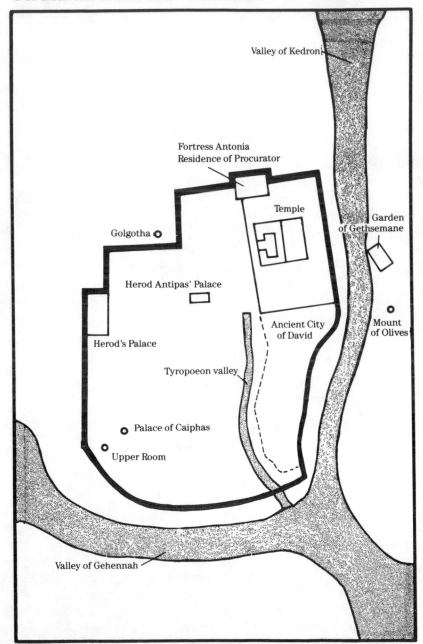

wanderings in the wilderness (Exodus 16:32; Isaiah 25:6-9) and reaffirmations of the leadership of the new Moses.

Mark weaves the wilderness theme throughout his gospel, and it takes on added significance because of the ministry of Jesus. The gospel begins in the wilderness of the desert and ends in the wilderness of the tomb. Jesus carries out large portions of his ministry in the desert, and seems to deliberately withdraw there so that people will follow him into the wilderness to be renewed. Mauser claims "The call to the wilderness is nothing less than synonymous with the claim of Messiahship."[4] The desert symbolizes not merely a yearning for solitude, but Jesus' constant call to the people to return to their original commitment.

The Sea of Galilee. The Galilean ministry takes place principally around the Sea of Galilee. In Mark, the sea is more than a geographical location. It is a place of withdrawal, revelation, and understanding; a dwelling place for demons and evil hostility to the Lord; and a barrier, or at times transitional zone, to new stages in the understanding of Jesus' ministry.[5]

Jesus' ministry begins by the sea of Galilee where he calls his first disciples (1:16-20), as later he calls Levi (2:13-14). The lakeshore becomes a place to teach by word and miracle (2:15-17; 3:7-12), and is the location of the parable discourse (4:1-9).

Just as the wilderness was a place of confrontation with Satan, so too is the sea (4:35-41); as Jesus rebukes the storm as he would an evil spirit. On the sea the disciples face their own need of renewal in faith (4:40) and appreciate the power, authority, and awesomeness of Jesus (4:41). In the strange episode of the devils at Gerasa, Jesus drives them back into the primeval and evil waters (5:1-14).

Although not itself a place of peace, the sea is often a place of transition to withdrawal and rest (6:32). In fact, without Jesus' presence, the experience on the sea becomes one of distress and anguish, but with Jesus it becomes one of greater understanding (8:14-21) and miraculous revelation (6:45-52).

The Sea of Galilee is also used as the focal point of a ministry that alternates between Jewish and Gentile locations. Jesus makes six trips on the lake, crossing from the Jewish to the Gentile sides, as he progressively shows how his ministry is available for both Jews and Gentiles. Trips across the lake, a place of fear and evil, become occasions for a clarification of his teachings and a reaffirmation of faith.[6]

Mountain.   Hills and mountains surround Galilee and Jerusalem, so it is natural to find the events of Jesus' life located on the higher ground. However, mountains recall theophanies of the Old Testament, major revelations of God, and important experiences of prophetic call, as do Sinai, Horeb, and Carmel (Exodus 24:12-18; 1 Kings 19:9-18). In fact, mountains also symbolize the stability and power of God.

In Mark, Jesus ascends the mountain to appoint the Twelve (3:13-19), an event that recalls Moses and the twelve tribes. On other occasions Jesus goes to the mountain for personal prayer (6:46). At a critical point in his ministry, after the confession of Peter and his rejection of suffering, Jesus ascends the mountain and is transfigured in the presence of Moses and Elijah, two predecessors whose own ministry was authenticated in mountain encounters with God (9:2-8; Exodus 19:16-25; 1 Kings 19:1-18). This episode becomes a new Sinai event in which Jesus takes on the central significance.

The theme of the mountain recurs when Jesus arrives in the region of Jerusalem (11:1). From the Mount of Olives he can look toward Jerusalem and ponder the events ahead, just as the next day from the same mountain he can look toward the desert and the Dead Sea (11:23) and challenge the faith of his disciples. At the conclusion of his Jerusalem ministry, Jesus departs, and again from the Mount of Olives, looks across at the city and its temple and thinks about the consequences of its rejection of his coming (13:3-4). Jesus frequents the Mount of Olives during his stay in the capital, and returns there after the Last Supper (14:26).

Thus, for Mark the mountain is another place of revelation, divine presence, call, and vindication. It is also the place from which Jesus judges Jerusalem and foresees the consequences of its rejection of him.

Galilee and Jerusalem.   Jesus comes from Galilee, ministers throughout the region, and calls his disciples there. It is the base of Jesus' ministry, and if he does leave from time to time, it is also true that others journey to Galilee to hear him (3:7-8). The main problems he encounters in Galilee do not originate there, but are provoked by leaders who come from Jerusalem (3:22; 7:1). When Jesus goes to Jerusalem he is accompanied by Galileans (15:41), and after his resurrection instructs them to go back to Galilee to meet him again (16:7). As we shall see in the next chapter, some writers are so impressed by the Galilean emphasis of Mark that they believe the Gospel was possibly written there. If there is in Mark a Holy Land or a Christian Land, it is Galilee.[7] This is so despite the fact that faithful Pharisees looked down on Galilee because of the presence there of Gentile and Hellenistic influences, and the lack of scrupulous observance among its people.

Galilee is contrasted with Jerusalem. The leaders of the latter are presented as legalists, narrow minded, and hypocritical. While the ordinary people seek renewal of life (1:5; 3:8), their leaders try to trap Jesus (3:22), argue with him (8:11), and are criticized for their insincerity (8:15). Above all, Jerusalem is the place of expected suffering (10:33-34).

When Jesus arrives in Jerusalem he is welcomed by a small crowd, but by the time he gets to the temple, he seems unnoticed (11:11). The next day on his way back to the city,   he curses the fig tree—an action symbolic of the destruction of Jerusalem (11:12-14).[8] His ministry in the city is short, and there seems to be a strange coldness between Jesus and the city.[9] He cleanses the temple, confronts the authorities, and prophesies the destruction of the city and temple (13:1-23).

During the passion, Jesus is tried and condemned by the Jewish leaders, and Pilate accedes to their request. Mark makes no reference to Herod Antipas, governor of Galilee, as Luke does (Lk 23:6-12). Rather, the entire blame lies with Jerusalem and its authorities. The death of Jesus brings to a climax the polemic against Jerusalem with the tearing of the temple curtain, symbolizing the end of the cult and its influence on people's lives.

The World of Markan Christianity

Mark wrote his gospel between 65-70, but probably before the fall of Jerusalem in the year 70. He wrote outside of Palestine in an area where Christians were undergoing persecution by the Romans. Tradition has generally suggested Rome as the place of origin, and this is still the most convincing opinion today. The gospel addresses a Christian community largely of Gentile origin, outside of Palestine, possibly living in or anticipating persecution. The community expects the fall of Jerusalem and some negative repercussions for themselves.

The land of Jesus is important because of the community's roots, but Mark writes at a theological turning point, when Christians are becoming more aware of their independence from Judaism, of the need to reject the distinctions between Jews and Gentiles, and of the challenge to think of worldwide mission rather than of mere regional expansion.

The world of Markan Christianity is the world of the Roman empire, with its power and control, its corruption and intrigue, its hybrid philosophies and mystery religions.

The Roman Empire.   The first Roman leader to receive the title emperor was Octavian in 27 BCE. For five hundred years before Octavian, the period of the republic (509-27 BCE), Rome was governed by the Senate, and in the centuries before the republic, there were kings (753-510). Octavian, who had defeated Anthony and Cleopatra in 31 BCE at the battle of Actium, was a wise ruler who brought peace and stability to the empire. Octavian was given the titles "princeps," or first citizen, "Augustus," a title which led some to consider him as semi-divine, and "pontifex maximus," or high priest. The reign of Augustus was a time of peace, consolidation of Rome's control over the empire, administrative reorganization, and tax reform. His legislation also included moral and religious reforms of decadent Roman life. Augustus was emperor at the time of Jesus' birth; he ratified the will of Herod the Great, and the cities of Caesarea Philippi and Sebaste were named for him.

Octavian, generally known as Caesar Augustus, died in 14 CE and was succeeded by Tiberius (14-37), his wife's son by a previous marriage. This is the emperor who ruled during the later life and entire ministry of Jesus. His early military and diplomatic career was outstanding, but he spent the last eleven years of his life on the island of Capri, fearing possible assassination. The prefecture of Pontius Pilate (26-36), one of Tiberius' appointees, coincides with this odd period of withdrawal in Tiberius' government. Herod Antipas built his capital on the shores of Lake Galilee and named it Tiberias to honor the emperor.

At his death in 37, Tiberius was succeeded by his grandnephew, Gaius Caligula (37-41), a capricious tyrant whose cruelty brought about his own assassination in 41. Gaius Caligula banished Herod Antipas, governor of Galilee, to Gaul in 39, and provoked a major crisis in Jerusalem by demanding that his statue be set up in the temple—a crisis averted by his death.

Gaius Caligula was succeeded by his uncle, Claudius (41-54), considered weak by those around him, but actually a competent ruler who challenged the senate to take its responsibilities seriously. He was probably poisoned by his fourth wife, Agrippina, in order to further the career of her own son, Nero, who became emperor in 54.

Nero was wicked and cruel, and within five years had, among other crimes, arranged the murder of his own mother. In 64, a great fire in Rome diverted attention from Nero's ineffectual administration and economic crises. Many, including the writer Tacitus, suggested Nero started the fire and later blamed it on the Christians. As we shall see in the next chapter, many gospel commentators consider that this period of fear and persecution is the context of Mark's gospel. Nero was eventually forced to flee Rome, and hearing that the Senate had condemned him to death, he committed suicide in 68.

A period of unrest followed, and the year 69 is referred to as "the year of the four emperors": Galba, Otho, Vitellius, and Vespasian. Only the last named was able to establish control and eventually ruled for a decade (69-79). He suspended his attack on Jerusalem to return to Rome, and once he had consolidated his rule, he instructed his son Titus to complete the conquest of Palestine and the sacking of Jerusalem in 70.

This brief sketch lists Roman emperors who governed during New Testament times and whose government forms the backdrop to events in Mark's community.

Life in the Roman Empire.   The extraordinary conquests of Alexander the Great (336-323 BCE) were not only military and political, but also cultural. Urged on by his teacher Aristotle, Alexander strove to bring the Greek language and culture to the nations he conquered, and although political disunity returned at his death, Greek remained the common language of the former empire. Three hundred years later the political power was Roman, but the language and culture were still Greek. This had immense significance for Christianity, whose missionaries could preach in Greek throughout the Mediterranean, and whose writers could use Greek as a universal language.

The social class system of the Roman empire included the senatorial aristocracy, the equestrian order, plebians, freedmen, freedwomen, and slaves. These distinctions were based on legal status and wealth, but sometimes wealth could place the slaves in better positions than the free poor. The higher ranks of equestrian and senator required Roman citizenship, which was hereditary, or on occasion granted by the emperor for outstanding contributions to the empire.

Most of the wealth was in the hands of a few, and the Roman standard of living was only maintained by the many slaves. The beautiful estates of the wealthy contrasted with the crowded and badly built apartments of the poor. Political purges, increased taxes, and the decline of family life and a falling birth rate resulting from decadence and immorality gradually reduced the numbers of the wealthy. The gap widened between the few rich and powerful and the many poor and oppressed.

Education was available to large numbers of people and consisted in studying the works of the great writers. Although philosophy was not studied by everyone, people yearned for answers to the problems of life and to ways of controlling the forces of the universe. Some found answers in philosophy, others in magic, astronomy, or religion.

Octavian had been given divine honors, Caligula and Nero demanded them. However, most people were skeptical about all the gods and goddesses of Rome, and many turned to philosophy. Two philosophies particularly attracted attention: stoicism and epicureanism. These two philosophies, unlike gnosticism, rejected the dualism of Plato (427-347). Paul encountered both in Athens (Acts 17:18). Stoicism, founded by Zeno (c. 336-263 BCE), believed the world is ordered by divine Reason, or Logos, and unfolds according to a plan. Stoic followers were well respected for their simplicity of life, virtue, and moral uprightness. Stoicism, rejecting the meaninglessness of life and the power of fate, focused on human responsibility to contribute to world history by living according to nature through ethical integrity.

Epicurus (341-270 BCE) taught that the world developed according to fixed laws, and that people could free themselves from fear and anxiety by following their inner feelings in pursuit of true happiness and by avoiding any excesses.

Philosophy, even the eclectic forms, held little attraction for the common people of the empire, many of whom turned to magic, astrology, or mystery religions as a means of controlling the world and attaining salvation. Magic offered formulas to control the mysterious powers of fate; astrology offered understandings of predetermined events; the mystery religions, with the aid of secret initiations, promised direct contact with the gods.

A philosophical and religious movement that took many forms was gnosticism. Although the earliest gnostic writings date from the second century of the Christian era, many historians think its origins predate Christianity. Gnosticism is dualistic, views the world negatively, and considers that salvation is attained not by faith, but by knowledge, a knowledge that enabled the devout to rescue the soul from its imprisonment in the material world.

During the first Christian century there lived a hero who was thought to embody the power of God: Apollonius of Tyana, whose life was written by Philostratus (c. 170-245). Apollonius is an example of a "divine man," a philosopher-leader whose disciples see as a god whose presence is manifested in his power, miracles, prophecy, and teachings.

The world of Markan Christianity is the empire with its rulers, social problems, philosophy, and religious life. The first gospel, written for Gentiles, must be situated in the events of the empire during the last quarter of the first century.

History in Mark

The historical value of Mark's gospel. This first gospel was written about 65-70, and is based on the oral traditions of the community. Mark's own interests and theological motives play a great part in his selection and arrangement of material (note: see chapter 3). Moreover, the outline of Jesus' ministry and the content of his preaching are determined by Markan theological concerns. At a critical turning point in the life of the early Church, characterized by growing independence of the community from Judaism by threat of persecution from Rome and by loss of the apostolic figures of the Church, Mark chooses to write a gospel, not a history or a chronicle of the times of Jesus. He proclaims the history of salvation rather than narrating the specific chronology of the years leading up to Jesus' death. He divides the history of salvation into four periods: the time of preparation, presumed in the Old Testament, culminating in the ministry of John, the precursor; the period of Jesus' earthly ministry—a time of secrecy and suffering; the post-resurrection period—a time of understanding, revelation, and open proclamation, as well as suffering, persecution, and betrayal; and the final period of eschatological fulfillment, when the Son of Man returns in power and glory.[10]

Mark's is not a history of chronological accuracy—what is said, done, or achieved; but rather he tells us the significance of what is really happening—a more profound and at the same time more accurate account of history. He sees the events of Jesus' life, of the Church, and of his own time from the same perspective, that of God acting in all these events, revealing his will and saving his people. Mark's understanding of history determines his interpretation of the future of the Church and of discipleship. In fact, his gospel is primarily a source for the history of the early Church and only secondarily a source for the history of Jesus.[11] However, history is rooted in Jesus, whose career is the heart of God's revelation of the meaning of all life.

Mark's portrait of Jesus, based upon authentic words and deeds of the Lord,[12] continues the Old Testament model of history, where God acts in the events of his people's lives. Mark's theology of history presents God's deeds in Jesus as the central interpretation of history. Thus the life of the historical Jesus is essential for the faith of the Church,[13] and without digressing to dwell on nonessentials, Mark presents traditions which speak for themselves of the central salvific significance of Jesus' conflict with evil, suffering, and death.

Were the scientific methods of contemporary historians to be used to find factual knowledge of the historical Jesus, there would be a lot in Mark that would give them a slice of real life, a feel for the kind of person Jesus was, conviction regarding the main lines of his teaching, and an outline of his ministry, with its conflicts and successes. However, Mark chooses to use historical records as a gospel proclamation to his own community, and his intention is not to document the past but to direct the future of the Church.

History and faith.   Our historical knowledge of Jesus is the basis of our faith. We cannot separate the Christ of faith from the historical Jesus without our faith becoming empty and unconvincing. But we have seen that in Mark "history is subservient to theology."[14] His knowledge of the historical Jesus becomes "faith-knowledge," which includes acknowledgement of Jesus as Lord and Christ.[15] Mark's four periods of history are centered on Christ, whose revelatory life gives meaning to each one. Thus the first period ends when John, anticipating Jesus' end, preaches and is delivered up (1:14); in the second period, that of his ministry, Jesus preaches and is delivered up (9:31; 10:33; 14:41); and in the third period the disciples will preach and will be delivered up (13:9-13). The passion of John anticipates the passion of Jesus, which is not only historical, but is a revelatory insight into the expected passion of the Church. Thus, the history of Jesus survives as proclamation and as challenge to faith, and Mark presents "a kerygmatized history of Jesus," that is, a history which has become embodied in preaching.[16]

Throughout his gospel, Mark presupposes that his audience believes in Jesus as Lord, and believes that times of waiting are over and the period of fulfillment has come in Jesus. Mark is not an apologetical work, but a gospel, a synthesis of the good news his community already believes. Mark presents two levels of meaning and understanding: that of Jesus and his disciples who slowly become aware of the meaning of Jesus' life, and Mark's community who from the outset can follow the gospel in light of their faith-knowledge of Jesus. The disciples' struggles, misunderstanding, and weakness can be overcome with the faith-knowledge of Mark's community.[17]

Mark tells the history of Jesus with his own community's critical needs in mind. These needs do not seem to be ethical, disciplinary, or communitarian, since Mark does not contain this kind of material. Rather, Mark presents Jesus as historically addressing theological problems that Mark's community faces: the need of vigilance in view of oppressive conditions and imminent persecution; false christologies and false interpretations of discipleship; feelings of abandonment as a result of the failure of the Lord to return; pressures from apocalyptic expectations and messianic pretenders; concerns about evil, sin, and the power of Satan. The Markan Jesus addresses questions such as these in the Galilean controversies (2:1-3:35) and the two discourses (4:1-34; 13:1-37). Aware of the values rooted in the historical life of Jesus, Mark allows the historical Jesus to address his community's newly risen problems, thirty years after the death of Jesus. Thus the central revelatory insights of the historical Jesus become the measuring rod for Mark's community for whom the historical Jesus is now the Christ of faith.

History, faith, and prophecy. Mark's first period of history, that of the Old Testament culminating in the appearance of John the Baptist, anticipates the central period, that of Jesus' life and ministry. The third period, that of the post-resurrection Church, is modeled on the revelation of Jesus' life. The fourth period is inaugurated with the return of the Son of Man in power and glory. Chapter thirteen, seen by some commentators as a small apocalypse, and by others as a farewell discourse, "unites prophecy concerning the future with exhortation regulating the conduct of the disciples in the period when the Master will no longer be with them."[18] Written in the form of prophecy, it narrates future history for those who believe. In fact, history, faith, and prophecy are intimately connected for Christians. Faith gives understanding of history and prophecy. History seen in faith becomes prophetical of future life. Prophecy seen in faith becomes a continuation of history.

While the time of the prophesied end is not known even to the Son (13:32), it already affects the present. "For Mark the driving force in history is the divine power of the end of time, operative already in the history of Jesus, propelling the whole course of history toward its ultimate destiny."[19] The Kingdom, which came with Jesus, is finally established by the Son of Man, the suffering servant of the Lord, who is exalted and glorified. Thus the intrinsic relationship between passion and glory, in this case passion and parousia, is established yet again. What history anticipated in the Old Testament, confirmed in the life of Jesus, and proclaimed to disciples, is now affirmed for all: that glory comes through suffering. "The incisive promise, 'you will see,' repeated three times (8:38-9:1; 13:26; 14:62), can only refer to an open and definitive unveiling of what God has kept concealed."[20] Thus the fourth period of history confirms the other three. The eschatological vision is both the point of arrival of history and the point of departure for understanding history.

This chapter has studied the world of Markan Christianity: the ministry of Jesus which becomes the basic structure for the gospel; the land of Jesus, its place in the empire, its geographical and political divisions. We then view Mark's use of geography and the importance to him of concepts such as wilderness, sea, mountain, Galilee and Jerusalem. Since Mark's world is the Roman empire, we review its history and life. Finally, we reflect on Mark's understanding of history and its relationships to chronology, faith, and prophecy. With the background provided by these two chapters, we turn now to the reason Mark wrote his gospel.

Chapter Three
MARK'S PURPOSE

No one sews a patch of unshrunken cloth on an old
cloak. If he should do so, the very thing he has used
to cover the hole would pull away—the new from
the old—and the tear would get worse. Similarly,
no man pours new wine into old wineskins. If he
does so, the wine will burst the skins and both wine
and skins will be lost. No, new wine is poured into
new skins. (Mk 2:21-22)

After centuries of neglect Mark's gospel has received a lot of
attention since the mid-fifties. Although many recent commentaries have appeared, a lack of consensus remains regarding
Mark's purpose. When Mark wrote, the main body of the early
Church no longer expected the immediate return of the Lord;
nevertheless it seems unlikely that Mark is compiling the records
in anticipation of an extended future Church. Admittedly, the
apostles were dying, and there was concern not to lose the traditions, but Mark's work is a complex theological synthesis, not a
chronicle of past events; it is a subtle reflection, not a mere compiling of traditions; it portrays a sense of urgency and challenge
far greater than necessary simply as a result of the passing of the
generation of eyewitnesses.

Mark's gospel shows little interest in chronology or geography,
and is not an accurate account of the historical ministry of Jesus.
Because of this, Matthew and Luke show no scruples about changing the order of events, their location, and their audiences, for
even at this early date, Mark's readers understand that he is not
writing history, even though his work is rooted in historical events.

Mark's purpose is not exhortation or edification. In places his
text is quite unedifying, as for example, the misunderstanding of
the apostles, their lack of faith, their competition for places of
honor, or their final abandonment of the Lord. Mark's portrait of

Jesus includes impatience, anger, and other human reactions that Matthew and Luke will consider inappropriate. Jesus' passion, which Mark prepares us for at length, is described briefly without distress or compassion. The fleeing disciples are never presented as repenting or being reinstated in the Lord's chosen group. This gospel is hardly a work of edification, rather it leaves the reader with doubts, questions, and frustration.

Mark's gospel is not simply a theological synthesis of Jesus' life and mission. He chooses his material for its relevance to the redemptive work of Jesus, but this is then interpreted for its significance to the needs of Mark's community. To study Mark with "almost exclusive concern for the christological problem is not asking the right questions."[1] Mark is above all addressing Christian communities of his own time; portraying the significance and relevance of Jesus to their needs.

Mark is not simply "a passion narrative with a long introduction" (M. Kähler). In fact, the passion consists of only a sixth of the narrative, and while the elements of suffering Messiah and suffering discipleship are frequent themes, they do not adequately account for Markan structure, concerns, or interests.

I further doubt that Mark's purpose is exclusively apocalyptic. Chapter thirteen is a crucial section, and apocalyptical themes weave their way through the entire narrative. But the second gospel has many other interests besides apocalyptic, and in places even signals rejection of apocalyptical expectations.

A unifying aim is difficult to find, for Mark functions at several levels and affects different people in different ways. In this third chapter, we will consider Mark's interests, his special compositional features, and his unusual but frequent challenges to authority. All these components of the second gospel indicate that whatever the content of Mark, it is being proclaimed to disciples in periods critical for themselves and their communities. His gospel is a challenge calling for quality discipleship in times of uncertainty.

Mark's Interests

Gospel proclamation.   Mark starts his work with "Here begins the gospel of Jesus Christ, the Son of God," a simple but powerful opening statement. "Here begins" recalls the involvement of God in the first creation, and now in the new creative work of redemption. This is an important concept, a technical term in the early Church, used with theological intent by all the evangelists. Mark begins the narrative of Jesus Christ, the truth about him, and his significance to the community's need. This beginning, recalling the creation stories, indicates that a new era in human history begins with Jesus. Although the beginning is good news, it actually focuses immediately on John the Baptist proclaiming in the wilderness a message of renewal and identifying the Lord to come. John is at once an Elijah preceding the Lord, and the anticipation of Jesus' own calling, mission, and death. The beginning is hopeful, but points to the sufferings ahead.

Mark calls his work "gospel." Of all four evangelists, he alone uses this description. He proclaims the beginning of good news at a time when the Jews are anticipating the possible end of their nation and temple. Essentially the beginning of the good news is the arrival of Jesus to proclaim the kingdom, but as we read on, we find that the kingdom also proclaims who Jesus is for us.

Relating the beginning of good news, Mark hopes to explain to his community the meaning of their present situation. The opening is abrupt, presents Jesus already as an adult, even though Mark had other traditions available (6:3), and is silent on topics for which the early Church had traditions. In the narratives ahead Mark will give little sermon or discourse material, for the good news is not so much "the content of what Jesus says and does, but the power of Jesus himself, present where his story is told."[2] Mark throughout his gospel proclaims the power of Jesus seen in foundational events of the past, but alive and available to the community now.

This opening phrase is the fundamental theological conclusion of the gospel, anticipated in a creedal statement before the events leading to it are described. The whole gospel is a witness document, a proclamation of joyful news for Jews (8:29) and Gentiles (15:39). Although other community issues will be integrated, the proclamation of Jesus as Christ and Son of God will be a recurring emphasis of Mark in the confessions (8:29;15:39) and in the rhetorical questions.

Since Mark's gospel is based on traditions of the communities, the content is not new to the people. It is not a first time proclamation, but rather a reminder, a restoring of the past's authentic proclamation to disciples who Mark seems to think have digressed from it.

Some authors see Mark's sense of proclamation prolonged through his catechetical and liturgical concerns. P. Carrington considers Mark's sequence as following a Christian liturgical calender designed to be read a section at a time from New Year to September. J. Bowman views Mark as a collection of readings, a Christian Passover Haggadah.

Other commentators, impressed by Mark's practical arrangement of the proclamation, see him as a Christian scribe passing on the message of his master. His grouping of material (9:48-50; ch. 10), critical assessment of positions, and clear formulation of creedal statements (8:29; 9:31; 10:33-34) seem so useful for catechetical instruction that others think this was his purpose.[3]

Guided by the needs of his Church, Mark proclaims the perennial good news to disciples who have heard it before. He calls them to self-criticism, to authentic interpretation, to choice motivated by faith, and asks them to remember the dynamic presence of the Lord, alive both in the past and in their present time of need.

Recurring themes. Mark, the shortest gospel, is still a rich collection of early Church traditions, covering a wide range of interesting issues. While attempting to answer Church needs, his work shows consistent interest in a series of important topics. His three main focuses are christological, ecclesiological, and pastoral.

The words and works of Jesus are the central theme. Jesus is portrayed as very human (3:5; 6:3; 7:34; 8:12; 9:36; 10:13, 16, 21; 15:34), but also as a miracle-worker. He is rabbi, prophet (6:4; 8:28), Lord (7:28), Christ (1:1, 24; 8:29; 9:41; 12:35; 13:21; 14:61; 15:32), Son of Man, and Son of God. However, he is also in conflict with the Jerusalem authorities, his family, and his disciples. He insists on silence regarding his identity, and on the need for his suffering and death—an insistence his disciples cannot understand. He foretells his resurrection and return, but no one except a few fearful women witness the former, and the latter is left unclear. Mark's christological themes are frequently mentioned, but leave the reader with more questions than answers.

His ecclesiological focus is seen in several recurring themes. Starting with the kingdom of God, he gives us the first collection of parables. He portrays Jesus as gathering the initial group, providing rituals for them, sharing his ministry with them, and sending them out on mission. He seems to react against false eschatological

hopes in the Jerusalem Church, and focuses his support on a
Galilean-based Church. He signals the break from Judaism and
the necessity of the Gentile mission. It is a synthesis that contains both challenge and conflict.

A third recurring interest is the pastoral concern for his disciples. A sense of urgency is felt throughout the narrative—an
urgency to commit oneself to the Lord in discipleship. Frequently,
however, the special teachings on discipleship are given in
private, even secretly, and provoke confusion in the reader's
mind: is the call universal or only for a small group of insiders?
This confusion is intensified when it becomes increasingly evident that these insiders experience conflict among themselves
and frequently take a stance in opposition to the Lord.

The presentation of these major themes is already indicative
of the tension and contradiction that permeates Mark. All the
themes are eventually woven into the passion narrative—adding
a further element of tension. Christ is Lord, but rejected by his
chosen ones; although his community is established with care, it
experiences much conflict; his disciples are carefully trained and
are the recipients of special attention and teaching, yet they still
end up in opposition. Mark's synthesis is unusual, his major themes,
presented with consistency, still leave questions unanswered.

Theological clarifications.   Mark's gospel is characterized by a
bluntness, a take-it-or-leave-it attitude which is rather shocking. As he proclaims his message, he recalls the past, asks that his
Church remember what it was really like, and reminds them that
the good news is painful too. Among Mark's interests is the
pastoral concern to clarify theological interpretations of foundational events and to return to the community's origins.

The predominant theological clarification that Mark weaves
through his work regards the nature of authentic messiahship.
On the one hand, Jesus was not just a rabbi whose teachings the
community passed on, but much more; he was prophet, Lord,
and Son of Man. On the other hand, he is not to be exalted as
cosmic redeemer at the cost of losing sight of his earthly ministry,
and so Mark for the first time in the Church gives a detailed
outline of the ministry of Jesus. Furthermore, some members of
the community seem to portray Jesus as a Hellenistic divine-
man, a wonder-worker who shares his power with his disciples,
but Mark contrasts this with his suffering Son-of-Man

christology. Moreover, the kingdom Jesus brings is not abstract but implies the need to build community—a position not all Mark's community accepts.

As Mark paints his portrait of Jesus he seems to correct several erroneous interpretations circulating in his community. Mark's community confesses Jesus as "Christ," but, seemingly, it is "a title that was too easily confessed, that expressed too little and was somewhat vague."[4] Mark's christology is clear and challenging: Jesus Christ is both Son of Man and Son of God.

Closely linked to the needed clarification of christology is the theological clarification of salvation. It is paradoxically achieved through losing one's life. Jesus did this (15:30-31) and reminded his followers of its necessity (8:34-38). In Mark the passion becomes the lens that draws everything into focus: it is the way to salvation.

In addition to authentic messiahship, Mark sees the need to clarify the nature of authentic Christian discipleship. Those members of the community, enamoured with the wonder-working powers of Jesus, see their own discipleship as a "self-actualization through the demonstrative use of awesome power."[5] Mark insists they must imitate the cross-bearing Christ (8:34-38; 9:33-37), drink from his cup (10:38), and commit themselves to a life like that of Jesus' suffering servanthood (10:35-44).

Mark must also call his Church to an awareness of their independence from Judaism. In the Acts of the Apostles the links with Judaism are maintained by the early Church, and even cultivated. Some remain "in the framework of Judaism," while "taking a liberal attitude towards proselytism of non-Jews."[6] Mark makes the break clear: the disciples are no longer Jews or Gentiles, but Christians, and must launch a mission to the world (13:10; 14:9).

As part of his theological task, Mark sees the need to purify traditions his community likes, but which are inauthentic. He reconstitutes the original message and presents it clearly. By the time he has finished, no doubt remains regarding his understanding of Jesus' life and mission, the nature of discipleship, or the purpose of the Church.

Compositional Features

The interests of Mark contribute to his general purpose. In addition, several of Mark's compositional features give insight into his general plan and purpose. In this section we consider Mark's use of the temptation stories, parables, the secrecy motif, and his general outline of the gospel.

Temptation stories.   Mark locates temptation stories at critical points in his narrative: the baptism and first acknowledgement of Jesus' messiahship (1:9-13), the transfiguration (9:2-8), and the passion: anticipated in the garden of Gethsemane (14:32-42), and culminating on the cross (15:27-39). The first episode lasts forty days, the length of the chosen people's desert wanderings; the second is after six days, which symbolizes the beginning of a new era; the third ends with the ripping of the veil of the temple, symbolizing the end of Judaism. In each case the scenes contain a confession of Jesus as Son of God (1:11; 9:7; 15:39), but each episode is preceded by Satan's temptations (1:13; 8:32-33; 14:38). In the first story, part of Mark's introduction to the good news, Jesus begins his struggle against evil. In the second story, Peter becomes Satan, tempting Jesus to an unacceptable lifestyle (8:33). Peter acknowledges only the power of Jesus (8:29) and not his need to suffer (8:32). Ironically, when he witnesses the power of Jesus' messiahship, he does not understand that either (9:5-7). The third story, that of Gethsemane and the passion, shows the sleeping disciples unwilling to wake up to the realization that Jesus is the Suffering Servant (14:37, 41), an unwillingness shared by the crowds at the cross (15:29-32).

Each account affirms Jesus as Son of God, but at issue in each case is the nature of Jesus' lordship and the difficulty of understanding his ministry. Peter rejects the suffering of Jesus, and later the sleeping disciples "symbolize the Christian community to whom Jesus comes as suffering Lord."[7] In each of these temptations Mark expresses his deeply felt concern at his community's previous unwillingness to accept the authentic tradition of Christ, and hopes the episodes will arouse them from their sleep.

Parables.   Mark has six parables, two rather long ones: the sower (4:1-9) and the wicked tenants (12:1-12), and four short ones: the seed that grows secretly (4:26-29), the mustard seed (4:30-32), the fig tree (13:28-29), and the absent householder (13:34-37).

Mark presents Jesus as teacher in the parables. Each of them addresses actual situations in the life of Jesus. Generally, the parables, as distinct from allegories, have one main teaching, and secondary details should not be given individual interpretations. In Mark the parables develop a sense of urgency to commit oneself in faith, the nature of the kingdom, the growth of God's life in us, an awareness of the final age, the judgement of God, and the need of vigilance. Each parable is integrated into the gospel to focus on the needs of Mark's community. He also adds two explanations of his own on the purpose of parables.

The parable of the sower (4:1-9), better called the parable of the seed, describes four ways of receiving the teachings of Jesus. It is followed by an explanation from the early Church (4:13-20); an explanation that presumes a community that loses the word through temptation or persecution, or abandons it because of their craving for riches, or their overinvolvement with the things of this world. W. Harrington concludes the explanation "came about because Christians discovered to their shock and sorrow the truth that few really believed Jesus' message."[8]

The parable of the seed growing secretly is exclusive to Mark (4:26-29), and shows how gradual is the development of the kingdom. Disciples should neither expect spectacular growth, nor be discouraged by the slow acceptance of the kingdom; neither seek immediate success, nor be overwhelmed by opposition and failure.

The mustard seed parable (4:30-32) has a similar message, but seems to presume current disciples' doubts that anything great could come from such insignificant beginnings as those of the Church. In the end, they are told, it will be great, and its growth is God's work, not theirs.

The parable of the wicked tenants (12:1-12), addressed to the chief priests, scribes, and elders (11:27), challenges their leadership and their unwillingness to accept Jesus because he was not the kind of messiah they expected. Its ending, "Finally they left him," indicates their rejection of the Lord's final, forceful, appeal, but may also anticipate the decision of some of Mark's community who are finding that Jesus is not the kind of messiah they thought he was.

The parables of the fig tree (13:28) and the absent householder (13:34-37) both deal with vigilance. Mark does not want his community to be caught sleeping like the chosen disciples were.

Mark adds his own explanation of the purpose of parables (4:11-12, 33-34). The Markan Jesus says he uses parables so that the crowds will not understand, "lest perhaps they repent and be forgiven" (4:12). The crowds are "outsiders," whereas the disciples, who are insiders, understand the teachings when Jesus explains it privately to them (4:33-34). This phrase is a typical semitic notion, it represents an inevitable consequence as if it were the purpose of an action. However, Mark is no longer speaking to Jews, and as we shall see later, he consistently shows that the disciples, here the insiders, fail to understand Jesus' message. How they receive the word, whether it secretly grows in their hearts, to what extent they become the new leaders of the people, whether they live in vigilance or let Satan take the Word, depends upon God alone and his transforming power in their lives.

Secrecy motif.   Mark's explanation of the purpose of the parables seems strange to modern readers. He says parables are meant to hide the teaching, whereas modern readers would expect them to be used precisely to reveal teachings more clearly. The meaning of the parables is kept from the crowds, and revealed to the disciples, but it eludes even them. These crucial teachings are shrouded in secrecy.

The kingdom is also left in secret. Not only do disciples fail to understand its nature after receiving private explanations, but they are even accused of hardness of heart (6:52; 8:17). When Jesus works miracles, demonstrations of the kingdom's power (3:23-27), he enjoins silence (1:44; 5:43; 7:36; 8:26) and insists "Not a word to anyone, now" (1:44). The very acts that prove the kingdom is at hand are kept secret.

Although a heavenly voice twice says we must listen to Jesus, he withdraws from the crowds and "wanted no one to recognize him" (7:24). Later, he left the district he was working in and "began a journey through Galilee, but did not want anyone to know about it" (9:30). When people sought him out, he went off to a deserted place (6:32). On one occasion, he even went to Tyre and Sidon, and "He retired to a certain house and wanted no one to recognize him" (7:24).

During his ministry Jesus frequently performs exorcisms, and the conquered demons acknowledge his messiahship. These opportunities for public revelation are blocked by Jesus, who silences the demons (1:25, 34; 3:11-12; 5:6-8).

Even the confession of Jesus' messiahship by Peter (8:29) and the Father's confirming theophany (9:2-8) are both followed by injunctions to silence (8:30; 9:9).

To these examples of secrecy can be added the astounding Markan claims that Jesus is misunderstood by his friends (4:40-41; 6:50-52), declared insane by his family (3:21, 31-35), in addition to being rejected by his own people (6:1-6). The gospel ends in a total rejection that is never corrected (14:50; 16:8).

The preeminent secret, as we have seen, regards the nature of Jesus' messiahship and suffering as a means of salvation. He teaches the disciples this several times, but they never grasp its significance.

Crucial teachings like the nature of the kingdom, the work of his ministry, the success of his miracles, the power of his exorcisms, and his own status as Lord are all surrounded in secrecy. How is it that Jesus, who came to proclaim "This is the time of fulfillment" (1:15), is portrayed as keeping it secret? What does this mean for Mark's community?

Outline of the Gospel of Mark.

Mark's gospel consists of five sections:

I.	1:1-13	Preparatory events in the wilderness
	1:14-15	Transitional passage: a summary looking ahead to the Galilean ministry and back to John the Baptist
II.	1:16-8:21	Jesus' ministry in Galilee
	8:22-26	Transitional passage: a Markan bracket
III.	8:27 - 10:45	Journey to Jerusalem: way of suffering
	10:46-52	Transitional passage: the second bracket
IV.	11:1-15:39	Jesus' ministry in Jerusalem
	15:40-41	Transitional passage: pointing ahead to the women at the tomb and back to the ministry in Galilee
V.	15:42-16:8	Jesus' burial in the tomb

This fivefold division is geographical and chronological; however, it is also an accurate literary division.[9] Part I, the beginning, deals with the desert: a place of emptiness, death, and demons. It presents John the Baptist, the witness to the Lord, and points forward to the rest of the book. Part V, the end, deals with the tomb, also a place of emptiness, death, and demons. It describes the women's witness to Jesus, and looks back over the whole book. Part II describes Jesus' ministry in Galilee, and is balanced by part IV, his ministry in Jerusalem. The central section, part III, deals with Jesus' journey to Jerusalem, in which he reveals the nature of his messiahship and the nature of true discipleship. This central section is bracketed by the healing of two blind men, indicating that the journey is the gradual healing of the sight of the disciples regarding the nature of Jesus and their own discipleship.

The whole gospel is structured in inverted parallelism, or chiasm, A B C B' A'. Parts I and V are balanced and speak of similar things; parts II and IV are similarly balanced, both dealing with the ministries of Jesus. The central section is the journey, and being the hinge in a chiasm, becomes a key to the interpretation of the whole structure of the gospel. Transitional passages link each section together, looking back over what has preceded and anticipating what lies ahead. This chiastic structure, centered on the way of suffering, is a deliberate Markan framework.

A detailed outline follows.

The Gospel of Mark

I. 1:1-13 PREPARATORY EVENTS IN THE WILDERNESS

1:1	Title and joyous announcement
1:2-8	Ministry of John the Baptist
1:9-11	Baptism of Jesus
1:12-13	Temptations of Jesus
1:14-15	Transitional statement
	- looks back to John
	- anticipates Jesus' work in Galilee

II. 1:16-8:21 JESUS' MINISTRY IN GALILEE

Early acceptance

1:16-20	Call of the first disciples
1:21-28	Enthusiastic reception in Capernaum
1:29-34	Healings in Capernaum
1:35-39	Search for Jesus; his departure
1:40-45	Healing of the leper

Controversies

Parable discourse

Ministry around the sea of Galilee

	- on Korban
	- on defilement
7:24-30	Healing of Syro-Phoenician woman
7:31-37	Cure of a deaf mute
8:1-9	Feeding of 4000
8:10	Journey to Dalmanutha
8:11-13	Pharisees demand a sign
8:14-21	Mystery of the loaves: misunderstanding of disciples
8:22-26	Transitional passage
	- healing of a blind man

III 8:27-10:45 THE JOURNEY TO JERUSALEM: THE WAY OF SUFFERING

8:27-30	Peter's confession
8:31	First passion prediction
8:32-33	Disciples misunderstand: Jesus' rebuke of Peter
8:34-9:1	The cost of discipleship
9:2-8	The transfiguration
9:9-13	The new Elijah
9:14-29	A healing: the epileptic
9:30-32	Second passion prediction
9:33-37	Disciples misunderstand
	- teaching against ambition
9:38-42	- teaching against envy
9:43-50	- teaching against scandal
10:1-12	Teachings on marriage
10:13-16	Teachings on children
10:17-27	Teachings on wealth
10:28-31	Teachings on rewards
10:32-34	Third passion prediction
10:35-45	Disciples misunderstand
	- teachings against ambition
	- teachings against indignation
10:46-52	Transitional passage
	- healing of blind Bartimaeus

IV. 11:1-15:39 JESUS' MINISTRY IN JERUSALEM

Jesus enters Jerusalem

11:1-11	Triumphal entry into Jerusalem
11:12-14	Cursing of unproductive fig tree
11:15-19	Cleansing of the temple
11:20-26	Cursing of fig tree explained

Teachings

11:27-33	The authority of Jesus
12:1-12	Parable of the wicked tenants
12:13-17	Jesus questioned
	- on tribute to Caesar
12:18-27	- on the resurrection
12:28-34	- on the greatest commandment
12:35-37	Jesus asks who is David's son
12:38-40	Jesus warns against the scribes
12:41-44	Jesus praises the widow's generosity

Apocalyptic discourse

13:1-4	Prediction of temple destruction
13:5-13	Beginning of troubles
13:14-20	Great tribulation
13:21-23	False Christs and prophets
13:24-31	Coming of Son of Man
13:32-37	Need of vigilance

Events leading up to the passion

14:1-2	Plot to kill Jesus
14:3-9	Anointing at Bethany
14:10-11	Betrayal of the Lord
14:12-16	Preparations for the Passover
14:17-21	Prophecy of treachery
14:22-26	The Last Supper
14:27-31	Prophecy of Peter's denial
14:32-42	Agony in Gethsemane
14:43-52	Arrest

Trial

14:53-65	Jesus before the Sanhedrin
14:66-72	Peter's denial

| 15:1-15 | Trial before Pilate |
| 15:16-20 | Mockery by soldiers |

The Crucifixion

15:21-26	Crucifixion
15:27-32	Taunting of the Lord
15:33-39	Death of Jesus
15:40-41	Transitional passage
	- anticipates the tomb episode
	- looks back over the whole ministry

V. 15:42-16:8 JESUS' BURIAL IN THE TOMB

15:42-47	Burial of Jesus
16:1-7	Appearance of young man to women
16:8	Conclusion

Mark's Challenges to Authorities

Opposition to Jewish authorities. Much of Mark's gospel portrays Jesus as drawing the people away from unworthy leaders and providing them with new ones. Political authorities, Herod and Pilate, abuse their power, make arbitrary decisions, and unjustly execute John the Baptist and Jesus. Both embody the worst of political arbitrariness, killing others simply to preserve their own positions of influence. However, Jesus' challenges are not primarily directed to political authorities, but to religious ones.

Early in the ministry the scribes and Pharisees appear as opponents of Jesus, criticizing him for presumed blasphemy (2:1-12), dining with known sinners (2:13-17), lack of fasting by his disciples (2:18-22), plucking ears of grain on the Sabbath (2:23-28), and healing on the Sabbath (3:1-6).

After the call of the Twelve and the acclamation of Jesus by the crowds, scribes arrive from Jerusalem (3:22), seemingly to examine Jesus, and they accuse him of working miracles with the help of Beelzebul.[10]

The Pharisees and their experts in scribal interpretation again arrive from Jerusalem and begin to argue with Jesus regarding their traditions: handwashing (7:1-8) and korban (7:9-16). Later they ask for a sign of Jesus' authority (8:11-13).

During Jesus' Galilean ministry the Pharisees and their scribes come from Jerusalem to challenge Jesus, they are always around, ready to find fault with him. However, they are never presented as respected leaders of the people. Their criticisms regard traditions of their elders not the scriptures, and "it is their theological thinking that Mark reproaches with departing from the Scriptures on which it was in principle founded."[11]

During the journey to Jerusalem the Pharisees appear again, questioning Jesus regarding his interpretation of the permissibility of divorce (10:2-12). When Jesus arrives in Jerusalem, Mark presents him as going at once to the Temple to denounce the abusive practices carried out there (11:15-18). This so-called cleansing is bracketed by the two stories of the cursing of the unproductive fig tree (11:12-14, 20-24).

Only once is Jesus questioned by the Sadducees, and that is regarding the resurrection. This takes place during Jesus' Jerusalem ministry (12:18-23).

Throughout Jesus' ministry, the ever-present Pharisees and their scribes criticize Jesus among themselves (2:8), complain to his disciples (2:16), protest the disciples behavior (2:24), tell others that Jesus is possessed (3:22), question Jesus about his disciples (7:5), ask him for a sign but only as a test (8:11-13), and ask Jesus a question, but really only to test him (10:2). Only once do they publicly confront Jesus, and that is when they also have the support of the chief priests, and they question his authority (11:27-33). Jesus counters with the parable of the tenants (12:1-12), but undaunted, they again try to trap him, this time regarding taxes (12:13-17).

The problems between Jesus and his opponents cover religious authority—ethical, cultic, doctrinal, the nature of the messiah, and the resurrection. More significant is "the range of issues within the Markan church that this material has been made to address."[12] Although the Pharisees, scribes, Sadducees, and chief priests are in positions of power and leadership, in fact, the establishment, they are presented as petty, legalistic, straitlaced, and spiteful. "The leadership these authorities offer in Israel evolves in the story as the opposite of leadership that is appropriate to God's rule."[13] The leaders grumble among themselves, while the crowds praise God (2:1-12); they complain, while Jesus shows mercy (2:13-17); they are negative, while Jesus is joyful (2:18-22); they are legalistic, while Jesus is compassionate

(2:23-28). They plot to destroy Jesus when he heals (3:1-6), and accuse him of blasphemy when he exorcizes (3:20-27). They insist on the letter of their traditions, while Jesus insists on the spirit of scripture's challenge (7:1-16). Blind to his miracles, the leaders of the Jews ask for a sign (8:11-12). Jesus rejects their leadership and warns his followers against their teaching (8:14-21), ignorance (12:35-37), and hypocrisy (12:38-40). Preparing for the Messiah, they do not recognize him when he comes (11:27-33), plot his arrest (14:1-2), bring him to trial (14:53-65), and demand his death (15:6-15).

Mark's portrait of religious leadership is a frightening reminder to leaders of his own Church, some of whom may well have been contaminated by similar attitudes.

Rejection of Jerusalem.   Jesus quoted Moses supportively (1:44; 7:10-13; 10:17-19; 12:28-34), and worked with the Jewish groups of the north. It is their leaders he rejected. Mark, however, does not distinguish between the religious leaders and the institution they represent: they are generally presented as coming from Jerusalem. Not only does he reject the leaders, he also rejects Jerusalem and its temple.

The cleansing of the temple, bracketed between the two episodes of the cursing of the fig tree, should be interpreted in light of the latter. The city and temple have been unproductive, and the withering of the fig tree symbolizes judgment on the city and temple, "withered to its roots" (11:20). Jesus' so-called cleansing, which is more appropriately described as a termination of the centrality of the temple, "not only puts an end to the temple's business operations," but "also suspends the practice of cult and ritual."[14]

The apostles, in awe at the temple's greatness, are told by Jesus that it is finished as a religious center (13:1-4), and its destruction at hand (13:14). Jesus' views on the end of the temple were also known to the people (14:58; 15:29). Its end is related to Jesus' death (10:33-34), and with it comes the beginning of a new way to God. At the moment of his death "the curtain in the sanctuary was torn in two from top to bottom" (15:38). The religious institution that guaranteed salvation is totally rejected.

So total is the rejection, that unlike Luke, Mark does not portray the early Church as reconstituted on the Jerusalem hopes. The future of the Church in Mark is away from Jerusalem, in

Galilee. The gospel started (1:16), Jesus worked his main miracles (1:23-2:12), chose his followers (3:13-19), and gave his principle teaching around the sea of Galilee (4:1-34). During the Last Supper Jesus asserts: "after I am raised up, I will go to Galilee ahead of you" (14:28), a directive reaffirmed by the angelic figure in the scene of the empty tomb (16:7).

Some writers have been so impressed by Mark's emphasis on Galilee, they conclude it is a Galilean gospel, written for a Galilean Church, encouraging the early Christians to leave Jerusalem and gather in Galilee to await the return of the Lord.[15] I doubt it is necessary to conclude the gospel is written for a Galilean community. Probably it is enough to point out that "Galilee symbolizes a freer spirit than that represented by the walled city of Jerusalem. The kingdom is open to 'all the nations,' Jews and Gentiles, as well as to both males and females. It is not hierarchical in structure but egalitarian in nature."[16] Jerusalem is not this, in fact it cannot communicate the message with which it is entrusted (16:7-8).

Confrontation with leaders of the Church.   Jesus' opposition to the Jewish authorities and his rejection of Jerusalem is easier to understand and interpret than is Mark's presentation of Jesus' constant confrontation with leading figures in his future Church. We have already seen the disciples' misunderstanding of Jesus' teaching,their inability to appreciate his way of messiahship and their rejection of the cross. While we can presume Jesus' support of his disciples (3:13-19, 34-35), there is no recorded word of praise for them from Jesus, whereas they are criticized for their misunderstanding (4:13), lack of faith (4:40), and inability to appreciate the significance of miracles (8:17-21). They have insufficient faith to work miracles (9:18, 28-29), are ambitious for positions of importance (9:33-37; 10:35-40), and envious among themselves (10:41-45). They forbid children from approaching Jesus (10:13), and try to control the ministry of others not in their group (9:38-40). In Jesus' time of need they are unable to pray with him, abandon him (14:50), and are nowhere to be seen at the cross. The disciples neither understand nor accept Jesus' teaching; their values are not those of Jesus, and at times their attitudes are closer to those of the rejected Jewish authorities than they are to the Lord's.[17]

Among the disciples, three are closer than the others to Jesus during his ministry: Peter, James, and John. These three receive special criticism from Mark. The three of them are with Jesus at his transfiguration, but fail to understand its real implication. After each solemn prediction of Jesus' suffering, one of the three is pictured with the opposite attitudes: Peter rejects the suffering (8:32-33), John seeks control instead of service (9:38-40), and James joins John in seeking status (10:35-37). In the garden of Gethsemane the three are again chosen but abandon Jesus in his suffering.

Of all the disciples, it is Peter who both occupies a leading role and is most negatively portrayed. Jesus gave Simon the name Peter—the rock, but ironically, he is very weak, cannot face suffering, falls asleep when needed, flees, and denies his master. Rather than a rock of stability, Peter is more like the rock on which the seed is sown, and where soil has no depth.[18] In fact, in the garden scene, Jesus returns to calling him Simon (14:37).

Peter confesses Jesus' messiahship (8:29), but this is only a partial identification with the Messiah Jesus is called to be, and Jesus ends up exorcizing Peter of his evil suggestion and half-hearted faith (8:31-33). Peter's inability to fully confess the Lord is seen at its worst during the trial, when he becomes ashamed of Jesus and publicly denies him (14:66-72; 8:38).[19]

Mark's polemic against the leaders of the future Church is continued in his harsh treatment of the close relatives of Jesus. Not only is Jesus rejected by his own townspeople—Mark says "kindred, and in his own house" (6:4)—but his family actually states "He is out of his mind" (3:21). The family's rejection of Jesus is heightened by Mark's use of another bracket technique. The two episodes on family rejection bracket the blasphemy of the scribes (3:20-21, 31-35 and 3:22-30). The episode ends with Jesus rejecting family ties and choosing instead faithful disciples (3:34). The episode has clear Markan editorial features and suggests his paralleling of the insensitivity of Jesus' family with that of the scribes. After this account, we do not see the family reinstated as a major influence in the kingdom.

Mark consistently confronts authorities that offer themselves as foundations for the kingdom: the Jewish authorities, the city of Jerusalem and its temple cult, the disciples, Peter, James, and John, and the very family of Jesus. Mark resists presenting any institution or group as having special rights and privileges. The common link between these groups is possibly the early power of the Jerusalem Church, based upon the Twelve, especially the triumvirate of Peter, James, and John, and later on possible family connections, especially with James. This Markan attack is only explicable in light of problematic leadership in his own Church that he feels obliged to challenge.

Directions for Times of Uncertainty

A persecuted community. Mark's Greek gospel is written for the Gentiles, and he explains to them Jewish customs (7:3-4; 14:12; 15:42), translates Aramaic words (3:17; 5:41; 7:11, 34; 10:46; 14:36; 15:22, 34), and gives some geographical information when he knows it (1:5, 9; 11:1). Since many Gentiles live in Galilee (Mt 4:15), this northern region could be a possible place of origin, and several commentators support this view.[20] However, this would not account for the explanations of Jewish issues. Other commentators, struck by Mark's frequent reference to places on the northern borders, suggest southern Syria, and see Mark "as a challenge and guidebook for the community whose members travelled as intinerant charismatics."[21] Trocme considers somewhere in Palestine as more likely.[22] The Greek Father, Chrysostom, appreciating the tradition that Mark was the patriarch of Alexandria, located the gospel's origin in that Egyptian city.

The firmest opinion of early tradition, also supported by the majority of modern scholars, is that Mark was written in Rome, or near Rome. While external evidence is scarce,[23] internal evidence points to Mark's gospel as written for non-Palestinian Christians of Gentile origin; it contains more Latinisms than any other gospel,[24] but is especially noteworthy for its description of persecution typical of that experienced in Rome consequent on the policies of Nero.[25]

The emperor Nero, faced with an internal economic crisis, diverted attention from his problems by burning Rome. The Christians were blamed for the disaster, and an era of persecution began. In this context, Mark presents Jesus' call to share in his suffering servanthood. Just as Jesus was with wild beasts in the wilderness (1:12-13), so the disciples are thrown to the wild beasts in the arena. Like Jesus, they too are misrepresented (3:21), betrayed (3:19; 14:10-11), and denied even by their friends (14:66-72). Moreover, although the faith of his closest disciples was never strong, the community knew that in the end they all proved their dedication by dying for their faith.

This uncertain time of persecution is not a time to save one's life, but to lose it for the sake of the gospel (8:35). It is not a time to expect miracles, for Jesus never wanted to be followed for his miracle-working power. It is a time to anticipate death, and while resurrection will come, it is not emphasized (16:7-8).

Some writers date Mark after the fall of Jerusalem, considering that chapter thirteen presumes it has already happened, and the gospel is a reaction to the loss.[26] Other writers offer a much earlier date.[27]

The most convincing date for Mark is around 65-70, most likely before the fall of Jerusalem. Any date earlier than 65 is not likely, since the gospel's discrediting of Peter is best seen as following his martyr's death in 64 or 68, and unthinkable before it. Chapter thirteen is appropriately accounted for in the crisis of the Roman occupation of Palestine after 67-68, with the fall of Jerusalem expected when Vespasian authorized it after gaining control in Rome.

There is nothing in the gospel that militates against 65-70, and this date also fits Nero's persecutions.

Questions of faith. Mark wrote at a critical turning point in early Christianity. Those who expected the immediate return of the Lord, as did some in Mark's community, were disappointed. Others, experiencing anxiety because of the death of the apostles, clung to religious attitudes they felt gave them security. Still others, fearful of persecution, needed to accept their suffering Lord, who called them to a suffering discipleship. While Mark's gospel does not readily reveal a unifying aim, there are several issues that focus in one direction.

In calling his work a gospel, Mark emphasizes that this is the good news his community should hear. Out of many traditions, Mark's work restores the past's authentic proclamation to a community that is losing it. He portrays a suffering Christ, the Church with a new mission, and a discipleship reserved for the small inner group who can penetrate the secrets of this new way. Of all the evangelists' communities, Mark's is the one that evidences the greatest disparity in their understanding of faith. Their choice is unquestionably for a comfortable religion with a miracle-working Christ like the divine-man of Hellenism, a discipleship of power, status, and self-actualization, and a Church with syncretistic practices that felt no need to break with Judaism. Mark must confront this watered-down version of Christianity, and give direction to a community that has lost impetus. He takes the community's present temptations, places them back in Jesus' time, and lets his community face Jesus' reactions to them. He reminds his community, in the parables, that the authentic teaching on which their lives are based is a revelation reserved for a privileged few, and they will be judged on how they receive these seeds of truth in their hearts. Their responsibility to value this special message is serious, and Mark puts his community in the role of Jesus' disciples, who show lack of understanding, weak faith, reject Jesus' teaching, and finally abandon him; he forces his community to confront their own attitudes to see if they are doing any better than Jesus' disciples did.

Mark in structuring his gospel centers the story on the way of suffering: a focus his community clearly needs. Jesus' ministry is divided into two main parts on each side of the journey section. The whole gospel begins and ends in the wilderness of the desert or the tomb, symbols of the emptiness, temptation, and possible death that await those who do not center their lives on the authentic way of the Lord.

Mark's work is a return to sources and a challenge to his community to get rid of the accumulated human traditions that distort the purity of the Lord's message. He rejects legalistic approaches to the faith, such as the fasting, rituals, and mechanical Sabbath observances of the Pharisees; an excessive concern with the importance of Jerusalem as the foundation for the Church; and any controlling influence over the faith, based on status, friendship, or relationship with Jesus. For Mark authentic faith is not assured by legalism, sanctuary, or position, but by the community's courageous self-criticism before the original call of the Suffering Servant.

Spirituality for a time of uncertainty. Mark's community, faced with persecution from outside, finds its faith severely tested. The Markan Jesus, primarily seen in hostile situations, encourages his disciples to face their own suffering as the principal way to God. He urges them to take heed, stand firm, and imitate his suffering ministry (13:9-13).

Mark's spirituality of suffering focuses on the essence of imitation of Christ. He prepares disciples to face persecution and unprecedented hardship (13:19). There are some signs of hope:

the message is good news, the kingdom is here, the Church will extend to the Gentiles. But oppression and persecution are integral to Christian existence.

Perhaps as painful as persecution from outside is the need to face watered-down and comfortable approaches to religion, and reconstitute the original rigorous call of faith. Mark is concerned that his community not lose the authentic tradition of Jesus, for it too can help them in times of uncertainty and persecution. He confronts complacency and unproductiveness, rejects culture's comfortable miracle-working Christ, opposes false teachers, even if they have authority, and calls the community to redefine its faith in the Son of Man.

Mark's spirituality calls for the constant purifying of faith, a return to sources, and an acceptance of insecurity in one's commitment to the Lord.

A further concern in his community is dependence on traditions, rituals, laws, and authorities; Mark challenges all to assume personal responsibility for Christianity. Jerusalem did not live up to the nation's expectations, Pharisees and scribes failed their people, the apostles abandoned the Lord, and friends and relatives proved unfaithful. Each disciple must take up his own cross and follow the suffering Messiah. Mark's portrait of the irresponsible disciples and women who although entrusted with the Easter message do not hand it on reminds each one that responsibility is personal and individual.

Christians who accept the suffering Lord, focus on faith uncluttered by inauthentic traditions, and accept personal and individual responsibility to pass it on, need also appreciate that it is a privilege to receive the message of Jesus, which is shared with only a few. It must be relished and taken to heart (4:20). Moreover, reflection on the events of Jesus' life and ministry leads to deeper understanding of faith and appreciation of Jesus. Although requiring understanding, faith grows secretly, the work of the Lord (4:26-29).

During times of uncertainty from persecution or theological differences, vying for power and control become common. Mark portrays the apostles squabbling among themselves (10:41-45), insistent in fighting for status (10:35-40), position (9:33-37), and control over others (9:38-43). Jesus calls them to mutual respect and service, and gives himself as an example to follow (10:42-45).

As we have already seen, Mark may have used a source

consisting of passages introduced with "Be on your guard!"
Whether he used such a source or not, vigilance is clearly an interest of Mark, and he frequently warns his community of its
necessity (13:5, 9, 23, 33, 37). In times of calamity from persecution or divisiveness, it is spiritually necessary to be constantly
vigilant; "Let no one mislead you" (13:5), hold out till the end
(13:13), "keep praying" (13:18), guard against false Christs and
false prophets (13:22-23), analyze the signs of the times
(13:28-29), "Be constantly on the watch! Stay awake!" (13:33),
"Do not let him. . .catch you asleep" (13:36), "Be on guard!"
(13:37). Thus Markan spirituality includes constant vigilance.

Future chapters will examine the spiritual challenges in
discipleship, ecclesial life, mission, and service. In focusing here
on the purpose of Mark, we see that he is writing in critical and
uncertain times, and to disciples he recommends a spirituality
that will sustain them, based on suffering, authentic faith, personal responsibility, understanding, service, and vigilance.

Chapter Four
MARK'S PORTRAIT OF JESUS

Immediately on coming out of the water he saw the
sky rent in two and the Spirit descending on him
like a dove. Then a voice came from the heavens:
"You are my beloved Son. On you my favor rests."
(1:10-11)

Mark narrates the good news of Jesus Christ, the Son of God (1:1).
He refers to God forty-eight times, using the title Father for only
two of them. He also refers to the Holy Spirit six times. His por-
traits of the Father and of the Spirit are simple, and generally
close to Old Testament usage. Certainly, there is no elaboration
such as we find in Luke.[1] Four of his references to God speak of
God as "Lord," two as "Lord God," one as "God Most High," two
as "Father," and one as "the Blessed One." Seven of the uses
refer to Jesus as "Son of God,"[2] and fourteen refer to the "reign
of God."[3] In addition to these frequent common uses, Mark sees
God alone as Lord (12:29), as good (10:18), as forgiver of sin (2:7),
and claims that with him "all things are possible" (10:27). The
temple is his house (2:26). He is the creator (10:6; 13:19), the God
of the patriarchs (12:26), and Lord of King David (12:36). He controls the end of the ages (13:32), and shortens the final sufferings
for the sake of his chosen (13:20). We should put our trust in God
(11:22) who gives us his commandments (7:8-9), his word (2:3;
7:13), his way of life (1:3; 12:14), and his good news (1:14). We
must give to God what is his (12:17), dedicate our lives to him in
sincerity (7:11), acknowledge his mercy (5:19), do his will (3:35),
love him with all our heart (12:30), praise him (2:12), and keep
united lives that he has joined (10:9).

Mark makes only six references to the Holy Spirit, seen by him
as the inspiration of scripture (12:36) and of Christians in their witnessing (13:11). The Holy Spirit descends on Jesus at his baptism,
the symbol of a new creation (1:10), and sends Jesus toward the

desert to face the temptations of Satan (1:12). We are told that Jesus will baptize in the Holy Spirit (1:8), and that blasphemy against the Spirit will not be forgiven (3:29).

As we have seen, Mark's portrait of Jesus includes deliberate corrections of false understandings based on power and the miraculous, as found in approaches like the "divine man." Mark also corrects a christology that detaches itself from the historical Jesus in order to present an ethereal Lord, as in the letter to the Ephesians. Mark's powerful portrait is a simple combination of a variety of approaches. He gives us the titles that the disciples used to express their faith in Jesus: some come from the Old Testament, such as Messiah, prophet, Son of David; others express a more exalted interpretation of Jesus, such as Lord, Son of Man, Son of God. Some of these titles come from Jesus, others from the disciples, and still others from the Church's interpretation of the meaning of Jesus' life and death. In addition to his use of titles, Mark's christology is based on the revelatory value of Jesus' ministry—his healings, exorcisms, and personal embodiment of the mystery of the kingdom. Part of the revelatory value of Jesus' ministry lies in the reactions of awe, faith, and commitment, expressed by those who encounter him. The Markan Jesus is always with his followers, and his challenges to them lead to their confessional responses. Moreover, Mark's portrait combines the faith of the Palestinian crowds with the faith of Mark's community. Both encounter Jesus, and the Markan christology is an integration of the faith of each. Thus, his christology is closely connected with his ecclesiology.

The Markan Jesus is a multidimensional figure. The historical ministering Jesus and the risen Christ of faith are drawn together in an insightful synthesis that affirms continuity with the human Jesus while leading to a faith beyond anything the community had previously formulated. Mark's originality is not in adding anything new, but in his creative synthesis of those aspects of faith already existing in the early Church.

This chapter presents Mark's synthesis by successively considering the human Jesus, the ministering Jesus, the teaching Jesus, the suffering Jesus, and Jesus as the Son of God.

The Human Jesus

Jesus' simple origins. Mark begins and ends by recalling the home of Jesus in Nazareth (1:9; 16:6). A demon recognizes the

healer as a man from Nazareth (1:24), crowds refer to Jesus'
hometown in the healing of Bartimaeus (10:47), and so does the
servant girl of the High Priest when she accuses Peter of being
Jesus' disciple (14:67). Although most of Jesus' ministry is
centered in the towns around the northern shore of the Sea of
Galilee, especially Capernaum, Mark records one visit of Jesus to
his own part of the country (6:1-6). This is not a successful return
home for Jesus. Although "he kept his large audience amazed"
(6:2), they disbelieve his power and reject his message. "Jesus'
response to all this is: 'No prophet is without honor except in his
native place, among his own kindred, and in his own house' "
(6:4). Rather than reflect on Jesus' amazing sermon in Nazareth,
all the townspeople did was question his work because of his
origins. "Where did he get all this?. . . Is this not the carpenter,
the son of Mary, a brother of James and Joses and Judas and
Simon? Are not his sisters our neighbors here?" (6:2-3). Mark
sadly concludes "They found him too much for them" (6:3).
Jesus' own family react in a similar way, trying to protect him
from himself. When ministering in the towns along the shore,
Jesus hears that his family has travelled to see him. They think
"He is out of his mind," and so they come "to take charge of him"
(3:21), and send "word to him to come out" (3:31).

Jesus travels around the towns and villages of Galilee, loves
the outdoors and especially the lake (2:13; 3:7). His sermons
reflect the interests of his people—sowing, harvesting, and
vineyards. His miracles are compassionate gestures to the
typically unfortunate of his time—leper, paralytic, possessed,
crippled, deaf-mute, and blind. He is happy to heal a friend's
mother-in-law (1:29-31), raise a dying child, and help an embar-
rassed woman (5:21-43). He likes to spend time with his friends
(6:31-32) and speak to children (10:13-16).

Jesus is from Galilee, whose people are more open-minded
than the Judeans. The latter are scrupulously law abiding, avoid
contact with the Gentiles, and their leaders are accused of being
narrow minded. Jesus loves the Law, but is not enslaved to
legalistic interpretations of it (2:23-28), and knows people's
needs come first (3:1-6). Moreover, he frequently travels to Gentile areas, such as Gerasa (5:1-20), Tyre, and Sidon (7:24-30).

Simplicity and openness characterize Jesus' life. He is a
Galilean, sharing the peoples' values and priorities. Exceptional,
he must struggle for acceptance.

His strong emotions. The Markan Jesus is very human. He shows an ignorance of events, and demonstrates human feelings and strong emotions.

When the woman with a hemorrhage touches the hem of his cloak, Mark tells us Jesus does not know who has touched him (5:31-32); Matthew, however, omits this suggestion of Jesus' ignorance (Mt 9:22). When the disciples, returning to Capernaum after the transfiguration, are arguing about who is the most important among them, Jesus is unaware of their discussion (9:33). Luke dislikes Mark's suggestion of Jesus' ignorance and changes it to "Jesus knew their thoughts" (Lk 9:47). When Jesus later admits that he does not know the time of the end of the world (13:32), Luke simply leaves this out (Lk 21:29-33). However, Mark is not afraid to include descriptions of Jesus' human limitations.

The Markan Jesus also shows human feelings and at times strong emotions, most of which will be omitted by later evangelists. The Markan Jesus is full of compassion and is "moved with pity" at the sight of an approaching leper (1:40-41), is delighted to put his arms around children (9:36; 10:16), and is moved to love for the rich young man's life of dedication (10:21).

When Pharisees watched to see if Jesus would heal a man with a withered hand on the sabbath, Jesus "looked around at them with anger, for he was deeply grieved that they had closed their minds against him" (3:5). When he visits Nazareth he again meets rejection, and their lack of faith distresses him (6:6). On another occasion, when the Pharisees test him, asking for a sign, "With a sigh from the depths of his spirit he said, 'Why does this age seek a sign' " (8:12).

Jesus becomes indignant when his disciples prevented the children from approaching him (10:13-14); he sternly warns a cured leper to tell no one (1:43); when annoyed, he criticizes the crowd, "What an unbelieving lot you are! How long must I remain with you? How long can I endure you?" (9:19). At times Jesus becomes impatient with his own disciples' lack of faith and understanding (8:17, 21).

In the garden of Gethsemane we see another side of Jesus' humanity. "He began to be filled with fear and distress" (14:34), and told the disciples "My heart is filled with sorrow to the point of death" (14:34). He then pleads with his Father to let the trial pass away, and asks the disciples to keep vigil with him (14:36-37).

Mark's gospel gives us a portrait of Jesus that precedes the reworking of Matthew, Luke, and John. His presentation of Jesus identifies deep human emotions of love, sorrow, anger, and fear.

His need to pray. Prayer is one of the clearest indications of creatureliness, when we adore, praise, and thank God, or petition God's aid for our helpless lives. Mark shows Jesus as a person of deep prayer, a further feature of his portrait of Jesus' humanity. The first time we meet Jesus is when he chooses to participate in the prayerful ritual of John's baptism (1:9), an event that concludes with a confirming theophany (1:10-11). This is followed by Jesus' withdrawal to the desert, and while it is not explicitly stated that Jesus prayed there, this can be readily presumed.

Jesus observes the Sabbath prayer of his people (1:21; 6:2), is often found in the synagogue, and although this was primarily a place to teach, prayer was associated with it (1:21; 3:1). Jesus also encourages others to observe the synagogue rituals (1:44).

Early in his Galilean ministry we see Jesus as a prayerful person. "Rising early the next morning, he went off to a lonely place in the desert; there he was absorbed in prayer" (1:35). When he feeds the five thousand, and later the four thousand, Jesus prays to God for the blessing of the food (6:41; 8:7). After a period of intense ministry Jesus makes time for prayer. "When he had taken leave of them, he went off to the mountain to pray" (6:46). Jesus conveys an awareness of his need to encounter his Father, an awareness reinforced in times of miraculous activity (7:34). When his disciples fail to cure a possessed boy, Jesus challenges their ineffectiveness in ministry, and tells them plainly, "This kind you can drive out only by prayer" (9:29). Thus Jesus' own life of prayer becomes a model for the ministering disciples.

The Markan Jesus' ministry in Jerusalem is a time of confrontation with religious authorities, of intense sharing with his disciples, and of tension and anguish as a result of anticipated suffering. This is also a time of deep prayer for Jesus. The day after his arrival in Jerusalem, Jesus drives the money-changers out of the temple, proclaiming that it must be restored to its central purpose as a place of prayer (11:17). After three days of intense ministry, Jesus pauses to prayerfully celebrate his last supper with his chosen disciples. Aware of his betrayal, it is a time of ritual self-gift, permeated with prayers of thanksgiving and praise (14:23, 26).

A climactic Markan portrayal of the humanity of Jesus takes

place in Gethsemane, where we also see the most concentrated presentation of Jesus' personal need of prayer (14:32-42). In Gethsemane, in anguish and distress, Jesus prays alone (14:32). He prays to his Father, Abba, with a unique filial expression of trust, with desire to be saved from the suffering ahead, but with resignation and recommitment (14:36). During his time of inner grief and loneliness, Jesus prays with insistence (14:39), but still remains alert and sensitive to his disciples' own need to pray (14:38). Gethsemane shows Jesus' filial and yet persevering prayer, his interior struggle to heed the will of his Father, and his prayerful acceptance of his mission and personal vocation.

The final Markan comment on Jesus' prayer is the cry from the cross in Jesus' moment of darkness and abandonment: "My God, my God, why have you forsaken me?" (15:34). In extreme loneliness and pain, Jesus still prays to God whom he experiences as ever present.

As we will see, Jesus' teaching on prayer is complementary to his own experience. His prayer-life shows the depth of human need experienced by the earthly Lord.

The Ministering Jesus

A ministry of revelation or secrecy? Mark's work is a proclamation of the good news that the times that people had hoped for have arrived in Jesus Christ (1:1-3 = Exodus 23:20, Malachi 3:1, and Isaiah 40:3). Publicly acknowledged by God as his Son (1:11; 9:7), Jesus announces that "this is the time of fulfillment" (1:15), appoints disciples as "fishers of men" (1:17), and sends them "to preach the good news" (3:14). When Jesus preached, "the people were spellbound by his teaching" (1:22; 2:12; 5:20), and he felt constrained to move around to preach to others, acknowledging "That is what I have come to do" (1:38), "I have come to call sinners" (2:17).

Jesus says his presence is reason for rejoicing (2:19-20), his teaching is like new wine (2:22), his doctrine to be publicly accepted (8:38). He claims to forgive sin (2:5), to be the Lord of the the Sabbath (2:28),to be a prophet (6:4),to have the right to interpret the law of Moses (10:2-12), and to grant eternal life for fidelity to his teachings (10:28-31). He accepts acclaim as a miracle-worker (1:40), as Son of God (3:11; 5:7; 14:61), as Messiah (8:29), and as Son of David (10:48). He heals the sick (5:34; 6:53-56), exorcizes evil spirits (5:11-20), raises the dead (5:35-43), controls nature (4:39; 6:49-52), and cleanses the temple (11:15-17). He prophesies the future destruction of the temple (13:2), Peter's betrayal (14:30), and his own death and resurrection (8:31; 9:31; 10:32-34).

Jesus' ministry was well received and "his reputation spread throughout the surrounding region of Galilee" (1:28), crowds gathered as soon as they knew he was around (2:1-2), people brought all their sick to him to be cured (6:56), and crowds were "overcome with awe" (9:15). Jesus himself manifests a sense of destiny, an awareness of his power, a conviction of the significance of his teaching, and a realization that his ministry will be continued by others.

The term "Messiah" (Christ) is used seven times in Mark (1:1; 8:29; 9:41; 12:35; 13:21; 14:61; 15:32), but Jesus' sense of messianic destiny is linked by Mark to a motif of controlled silence — a strange linking of revelation and secrecy. Jesus publicly claims to be the Messiah (14:61), allows certain messianic titles to be used of him, and even gives messianic significance to his own preferred title of Son of Man (2:10, 28), yet elsewhere he enjoins strict silence on his disciples regarding his identity (8:30; 9:9). His messianic power is witnessed in the miracles, but he requires from those healed cooperation in maintaining silence about his power (1:43-44; 5:43; 7:36; 8:26). As Messiah, Jesus puts Satan under restraint and plunders his kingdom through exorcisms (3:27). Some evil spirits acclaim Jesus (3:11), but he rebukes them whenever they try to make him known: "Be quiet!" (1:23-25); "He would not permit the demons to speak, because they knew him" (1:34); "He kept ordering them sternly not to reveal who he was" (3:12).

Although he came to announce the arrival of the kingdom (1:14-15) and was welcomed as a person of power (1:7-8), teaching authority (1:22), and outstanding reputation (1:27), Jesus does not make full use of his influence over the crowds. Rather he withdraws into hiding (1:45; 7:24; 9:30).

Although Jesus came to preach to everyone (1:38), he claims to do so in a way that they will not understand (4:11). His secret teaching is revealed to his disciples and painstakingly explained to them (4:11, 34). He reserves for them alone his teaching on the kingdom (4:10-34), on what defiles a person (7:17-23), on prayer (9:28-29), on his sufferings and glory (8:31; 9:31; 10:32-34), and

on the end times (13:3-37). The disciples, who elsewhere show
signs of intelligence and leadership, are presented here as not
understanding Jesus' message (4:13; 6:52; 7:18; 8:17). Their
ignorance is heightened by the fact that they are privileged to
witness important moments in Jesus' messianic awareness and
ministry (5:37; 9:2; 13:3; 14:33).

This secrecy motif in Mark can be exaggerated. Some teaching,
reserved to the disciples, is appropriate to them, given their
future roles. It provides advice and encouragement for their
future ministry, and explains important teachings. Some of the
crowd's blindness is symbolic of Israel's rejection of the gospel.
Jesus' silencing of the demons is typical of exorcisms in which
the powers of good and evil struggle for dominance, trying to
gain the upper hand through knowledge of each other's names.

Even with the above explanations, the messianic secret of
Mark remains a major editorial feature of the gospel. Mark's is a
work of revelation, Jesus clearly intending to be understood as
Messiah. Given the variety of Jewish schools of thought regarding the Messiah, Jesus, if he wanted his claims to be taken
seriously, would have to explain his understanding of his ministry.
The pervasive secrecy of Mark cannot be a historical feature but
must be interpreted as a Markan theological addition.

Interpretations of the Messianic secret.   The secrecy motif in
the gospel has come to be known as the Markan Messianic secret.
Although focused on Jesus' messianic claims, the secrecy actually
pervades the teachings on the kingdom too. Since 1901, scholars
have tried to explain the purpose of this Markan feature. In that
year William Wrede published *The Messianic Secret,* a work that
has influenced all subsequent Markan studies.

Mark's combination of revelation and secrecy is frequently
confusing, especially when those called to silence proclaim Jesus
more vigorously (1:45; 5:19-20; 7:36). Burkill warns against any
suggestion that "Mark carries out the idea of the secret with
perfect consistency."[4] After examining the data, Wrede concludes "a historical motive is really absolutely out of the question; or to put it positively. . . the idea of the messianic secret is a
theological idea."[5] Developed in a period prior to the evangelist,
and widely held in the circles to which Mark belonged, Wrede
considers that the secret is not traceable to Jesus, but is an
answer to difficulties faced by the Church in the post-Easter

period. The secret does not refer to the messianic self-consciousness of Jesus—a modern concept, out of place in Jesus' time—but is an explanation of why Jesus, whom the early Church acknowledged as Messiah, is not thus recognized until after the resurrection. Mark's community concluded that the messiahship of Jesus, which they claimed, was secretly revealed by Jesus to only a chosen few during his ministry, and was known by the supernatural evil spirits. Hence, Wrede concludes that the Markan messianic secret is not historical, but a theological attempt to explain the contrast between the rejection of Jesus by his nation and the Church's post-resurrection faith. Other writers since Wrede have interpreted the secret as a way of accounting for the rejection of Jesus.[6]

V. Taylor considers the secret "is not a hypothesis imposed on the records from without, but an element integral to the tradition itself. Jesus imposed silence because of the nature of messiahship as He considered it to be."[7] Few commentators follow Taylor's suggestion.

Others are persuaded that the secret is incompatible with the general purpose of Jesus' ministry and can be viewed as a contrast technique used to highlight the revelations of Jesus' messiahship—still so clear in spite of his urgings to silence.

Some commentators such as H. C. Kee perceive the secret in terms of Jewish apocalyptic thought, in which the eschatological figure is presented as partly hidden and not fully revealed until the end of the age. For Kee the secret is not invented by Mark, but is "a pervasive element in the community's understanding of itself" and its relationship to the kingdom.[8] As Jesus' message was misunderstood and kept secret but proved true in his death and resurrection, so the community's life of suffering and rejection will be vindicated.[9]

For Schweizer the messianic secret refers to the hiddenness of God, which "despite all its mighty manifestations, is not seen by the blind world, and is often misunderstood."[10] Only disciples who are willing to journey through suffering can appreciate the presence of God's power. Thus the secret focuses on a style of discipleship and urges believers to apply its challenges to their own lives.

Several commentators see the secret as a device to correct false triumphalistic christologies. "The 'messianic secret' motif occurs precisely at those points where the tradition was most likely to be understood to represent Jesus as a divine man with power to avoid any difficulty."[11] Kilgallen thinks the secret's purpose is to direct attention away from the person of Jesus and to focus on his words to which Christians needed to be recalled in Mark's time.[12]

The Markan Jesus, immersed in humanity's strengths and limitations, is not the immediate success story followers would like to think he is. The first great need early disciples have to address is the problem of explaining their faith in a rejected religious leader. They know that Jesus is their Lord, and that his life and ministry are messianic. They may have taken time to appreciate this, but after the resurrection the foundations of their faith are clear (4:22; 9:9). For others, they must answer whether their Christ of faith is in continuity with the crucified Jesus of Nazareth, and if so, what justifies their faith. Whatever the explanations of the messianic secret, they all credit the Markan community with facing up to this critical pastoral issue. While Mark's messianic secret becomes a distracting detail when Matthew and Luke use it, and while it is probably not traceable to Jesus, nevertheless, it remains a creative attempt to respond to the first great community crisis of faith.

The Teaching Jesus

"Good teacher." The rich young man who questions Jesus during his journey to Jerusalem calls him "Good teacher." This designation "is virtually without parallel in Jewish sources and should be regarded as a sincere tribute to the impression he had made upon the man."[13] While Mark presents a very human Christ who is at times misunderstood, he also consistently presents Jesus as an exceptional teacher. Jewish leaders in Jesus' time taught "within a group authority. . .within an official synagogue. . . within a 'canonical' text," but Jesus stands alone and teaches "outside this group authority. . .outside the synagogue. . .outside the 'canonical' texts."[14]

Although Mark's gospel is much shorter than Matthew's or Luke's, he gives more attention to Jesus as teacher than either of the other two synoptics. Achtemeier suggests that Mark sees Jesus' activity as teacher as "the central thrust of his mission."[15] Mark refers to Jesus as teacher twelve times, in comparison to Matthew's four references and Luke's six. The verb "to teach" appears seventeen times in Mark, all except four in Mark's own editorial compositions.[16] The designation "teacher" is given to Jesus by his disciples (4:38; 9:38; 10:35; 13:1), by strangers (5:35; 9:17; 10:17, 20), by Pharisees and Herodians (12:14), by Sadducees (12:19), by scribes (12:32), and by Jesus himself (14:14). It also appears in various forms of the tradition: miracle stories (4:38; 5:35; 9:17), sayings (9:38; 10:17, 20, 35), pronouncement stories (12:14, 19, 32), and the last supper (14:14), none of which are editorial.[17]

For Mark, Jesus is preeminently the teacher, an emphasis which neither Matthew nor Luke follow.[18] The Markan Jesus teaches in the synagogue and "the people were spellbound by his teaching because he taught with authority, and not like the scribes" (1:21-22). When he was walking by the lake, people came to him and he taught them (2:13; 4:1-2), as later he would teach in the synagogue in Nazareth (6:2), and to the crowds along the Jordan (10:1). Once when he came ashore and found the crowds "like sheep without a shepherd," he was moved to compassion for them and "he began to teach them at great length" (6:34). As part of his private revelations to his disciples, "he began to teach them that the Son of Man had to suffer much" (8:31; 9:31). When he eventually enters Jerusalem, he teaches in the temple daily (14:49), taking occasion to remind the people what scripture says about the temple as a place of prayer (11:17), and about the Messiah as Son of David (12:35).

What kind of a teacher is the Markan Jesus? At times he is addressed as rabbi (9:5; 11:21; 14:45), and acts like a rabbi, gathering his own disciples, and giving them private teaching. He debates the Pharisees with questions and counterquestions, a practice common among the rabbis (10:2-12; 11:27-33). He takes questions from the scribes (12:28-34) and from the crowds, giving replies based on the Law (10:17-25). He questions the Pharisees about their legal interpretations—halakah (3:1-6).

But Jesus is more than a rabbi. "He taught with authority, and not like the scribes" (1:22). On thirteen occasions he introduces his teaching with a phrase that indicates its reliability and authority. Variously translated as "Amen I say unto you," or "I give you my word," or "I assure you," this introductory formula is a completely new way of speaking, and highlights Jesus' own convictions regarding the value of his teaching. "As such, the Amen-formulation is not only a highly significant characteristic of Jesus' speech, but a Christological affirmation: Jesus is the true witness of God."[19] With a sense of independent authority, Jesus also attacks the legalism and hypocrisy of the Jewish leaders of his day (7:1-16) accusing them of clinging to human traditions and disregarding the essential call of God (7:8). He warns his disciples against their teaching (8:14-21; 12:38-40) and ends his ministry by claiming to supplant the teaching authority of the Jewish leaders (12:1-12).

In Mark's final section, the apocalyptic discourse, Jesus warns his disciples: "Be on your guard. Let no one mislead you" (13:5); "False messiahs and false prophets will appear" (13:22), and he goes on to assure them, "The heavens and the earth will pass away but my words will not pass" (13:31). The sense of astonishment that the crowds felt at hearing Jesus teach (1:22) permeates the whole Markan account. Jesus is the authoritative teacher. However, "for Mark the authority of Jesus' teaching resides not in its force of logic or the originality and profundity of its contents, but rather in the power inherent in him as Son of God."[20] Before Jesus' teaching ministry begins, a heavenly voice confirms the source of his authority (1:11), as later at the transfiguration, the same authority is stressed: "This is my Son, my beloved. Listen to him" (9:7).

Teaching with power and authority.   Mark's portrait of Jesus as teacher is closely linked to the miracles and parables. The power of his teaching is confirmed by the power of the miracles. The hiddenness of the parables' meaning echoes the hiddenness of the power of the teaching.

A third of Mark's material deals with the miraculous. Eighteen miracles are recounted — five miracles of nature, four exorcisms, eight healings, and one raising from the dead. To these can be added three summary descriptions of Jesus' healing ministry and one section on the significance of the exorcisms.[21]

Markan miracles are confirmations of Jesus' teaching authority. The crowd's amazement at Jesus' teaching (1:22 and 1:27; or 2:1-2 and 2:12) is reinforced by the enclosed miracle (1:23-26 or 2:3-11). Jesus' power as a teacher is thus exemplified in a miracle. Most of the miracles—fifteen—take place before the journey to Jerusalem, arousing awe in the crowds and focusing their attention and reverence on Jesus as teacher. Once the journey begins, and the followers and opponents are identified, the miracles decrease in number, and the teaching sections increase in length. Several of the miracles are directly related to Jesus' teaching authority: the healing of the paralytic and Jesus' power to forgive sin (2:1-12); the healing of the man with a withered hand and the nature of the Sabbath (3:1-6); the stilling of the storm and the call to faith (4:35-41) the healing of the Canaanite woman and the mission to the Gentiles (7:24-30). On other occasions Jesus links the miracles to understanding, not awe (6:30-44, 45-52; 8:1-10), and still other miracles are symbolic healings that teach the nature of discipleship (8:22-26; 10:46-52) and signify the end of the temple (11:12-14). In fact, on one occasion Mark actually calls a miracle "a completely new teaching" (1:27). Achtemeier concludes: "whenever a mighty act is performed, the power of Jesus' teaching is also demonstrated."[22] Stock concludes: "In his description of miracles Mark consistently moves from the miraculous to the kerygmatic."[23] When the disciples, Jairus, the father of a possessed boy, and Bartimaeus ask for miracles, they all refer to Jesus as "teacher" (4:38; 5:35; 9:17; 10:51; 11:21). These expressions of Jesus' messianic authority demonstrate his power over sickness, nature, and evil spirits. They teach more powerfully than words the nature of Jesus and the authority of his message. While recognizing the deliberate linking of miracles and teaching, Burkill rightly concludes "in spite of the evidential value, neither the miracles themselves nor the confessions of the demons exercise any discernible influence upon the insight of the people among whom Jesus works."[24] We have already seen that when demons recognize Jesus' power (1:24, 32-34; 3:7-12; 5:6-7), he imposes silence on those healed.

Jesus' teaching, confirmed by miracles, is also complemented by the parables which become prophetic words that describe the ways of receiving his teaching (4:2-9): like a seed, his teaching starts with a life that grows on its own (4:26-29) and spreads in an extraordinary way (4:30-32). His authoritative teaching now replaces that of the previous Jewish leaders (12:1-12), for the center of their religion is now destroyed (13:28). Those who accept Jesus' teaching must live vigilantly in anticipation of his return (13:34-37). Parables are another way for Jesus to articulate his understanding of the reign of God and his role in it as sower of the word. The parable discourse of chapter four, commented upon in the previous chapter, presents three examples of small beginnings that unexpectedly result in extraordinary growth.

Jesus' teaching too, although having a small beginning (4:30-32) and being rejected by many (4:3-9), will eventually produce a wonderful harvest. These first parables become prophetic of the career of Jesus, as the later ones are of the Church.

Jesus' teaching is rejected by many, a rejection figuratively presented in Mark's explanation of parables where he makes the outcome the purpose (4:11-12, 34). Two of the Markan parables are directed to those who reject Jesus' teaching, a third describes the result of national rejection, and a fourth warns even the disciples regarding their vigilant living of his teaching. Intimately connected, all the parables gain clarity from reflection on the parable of the sower. When disciples questioned Jesus about parables in general, he explained the sower (4:10-20). In fact, he explicitly stated "You do not understand this parable? How then are you going to understand other figures like it?" (4:13). The sower is essentially descriptive of the ways of receiving Jesus' teaching.

The Markan Jesus is a great teacher whose words of power are confirmed by his deeds, and symbolically portrayed in the parables. In the end, the teacher is the greatest of the miracles (9:2-8), and God's clearest parable. Thus the authority of his word and power are united, and they will not pass away (13:31).

The Suffering Jesus

The pain of ministry.   Mark's is the gospel of Christian suffering. Once the title of the work is given, readers are drawn into a "restless rush to the Passion."[25] Mark immediately presents John the Baptist, the forerunner of the suffering Jesus, referring to his arrest, since John's own passion and death will anticipate Jesus'. Having aligned himself with John (1:9), Jesus soon experiences the religious authorities' opposition (2:6-12, 16-17, 24-28; 3:1-6), even though he has been observant of the Law (1:44). As soon as the early controversies with the scribes and Pharisees conclude, "they immediately began to plot with the Herodians how they might destroy him" (3:6). Although he comes to proclaim a message of hope, Jesus is rejected by the authorities, whose malicious scheming anticipates the trial ahead (2:6-8; 3:6; 12:13; 14:1-2, 10-11, 44-45; 15:10). Rejected by the religious authorities, Jesus experiences the same treatment from his family (3:21, 31-35), and his townspeople (6:1-6). The pain of rejection in his ministry climaxes simultaneously with his own disciples' inability to understand the nature of his destiny (8:21, 33).

Opposition and rejection complement early hints of the passion (2:20; 3:6). The religious leaders' challenges increase (7:5-6; 8:11-13); Jesus' open confrontation of their hypocrisy heightens the rift (7:1-16), and Jesus even goes on the offensive (8:14-15).

In addition to these painful experiences in his ministry, Jesus demonstrates, especially from the journey onward, a realization of the sufferings ahead. His three separate predictions (8:31; 9:31; 10:32-34),[26] each made more painful by the disciples' obtuseness and unwillingness to accept the inevitable (8:32-33; 9:32-37; 10:35-45), indicate Jesus' own conviction and prophetical insight that his ministry will doubtlessly end in death. "The Son of Man has come. . . to give his life in ransom for the many" (10:45). Mark reinforces Jesus' awarenesss with a series of "death notices" that punctuates the remainder of the narrative,[27] provoking a crescendo of fear and distress in Jesus, who acknowledges "My heart is filled with sorrow to the point of death" (14:34).

Mark reinforces his portrait of the painful ministry of Jesus with his extensive allusions to the death ahead: the martyrdom of the Baptist (6:14-29); Jesus' post-transfiguration reference to the suffering Son of Man (9:9-13); the Pharisees attempt to force Jesus to make statements similar to those which led to the Baptist's death (10:1-12);[28] Bartimaeus' acclaim of Jesus as Son of David (10:46-52); the cursing of the fig tree to its roots (11:12-14, 20-21); and the open challenge to temple authorities, leading to a second plot against him when they "began to look for a way to destroy him" (11:15-18).[29]

Jesus' ministry brings rejection from all sides, a blindness to the nature of his life and work, malicious plotting by opponents, slanderous accusations against his ministry (3:22-27), fearful foreboding (6:14-29), and a general abandonment of Jesus to a lonely acceptance of his destiny. The pains of labor, prophesied in the farewell address on Olivet, describe well the anticipated end of Jesus' own ministry: handed over, beaten, arraigned before governors, betrayed by a brother, hated, and put to death (13:9-13). For Mark, the shadow of the cross "falls across the entire span of Jesus' ministry."[30]

The anguish of the last days. The passion account shows as much Markan editorial activity as the rest of the gospel.[31] The basic components of the passion tradition, already fixed in the community, are creatively shaped by Mark into the account we now have. Markan style, constructions, and theology permeate chapters 14-16.[32] Consisting of about fifteen percent of Mark's gospel, the passion account is both the inseparable climax of the narrative and the key to the interpretation of the entire proclamation.

Jesus journeys to Jerusalem aware that he will encounter authorities who oppose him and have plotted his destruction from the first stages of his ministry in Galilee (3:6). At the end of his second day in Jerusalem these same authorities are again plotting Jesus' destruction (11:18), by the third day they are looking for ways to kill him (14:1-2), and Judas, "one of the Twelve," is willing to hand him over (14:10-11). The two episodes on the death plot and betrayal enclose the only gesture of love and compassion that Jesus receives in Jerusalem: his anointing for death, not by a known disciple, but by an unknown woman (14:3-9).

The early part of Jesus' fourth day in Jerusalem is spent with his disciples, preparing for the Passover supper.[33] The special meal, the third in the gospel (6:34-43; 8:1-9; 14:22-25), portrays Jesus' undaunted commitment to his weak disciples, and symbolizes his mission to feed humankind. This solemn, selfless, ritual meal in which all the disciples share Jesus' cup is surrounded by two further examples of the disciples' persistent blindness, weakness, and failure: the betrayal by Judas (14:17-21), the prophesied abandonment by the Twelve, and the denial by Peter (14:27-31). Peter, who had rejected the very idea of suffering (8:32), "kept reasserting vehemently, 'Even if I have to die with you, I will not deny you' "(14:31). Preparing us for what is to come, Mark ironically adds "They all said the same."

Leaving the supper room, they all go to Gethsemane. This episode "marks Jesus' last attempt to resolve the conflict between him and the disciples. But instead of the hoped-for reconciliation, Mark reports a final parting of the ways" (14:32-42).[34] In agony, abandonment, and loneliness, Jesus rededicates himself to his Father's mission (14:36), while the apostles who had expressed their willingness to die, undergo temptation, do not pray, cannot even stay awake, and fail miserably. Enthusiastic for a short while (14:31), "When some pressure or persecution overtakes them because of the word, they falter" (4:17). The disciples' rejection of a suffering Messiah reaches its cruelest expression as they disinterestedly sleep while the Lord they had seen on Tabor faces the fear and distress caused by the thought of the suffering ahead.[35] The garden scene ends when "one of the Twelve...The Betrayer" hands Jesus over to his enemies (14:43-45), and all the other apostles "deserted him and fled" (14:50). Comforted and strengthened by his Father, Jesus turns to the trials ahead.

The Sanhedrin trial which follows presents many discrepencies with approved rabbinical procedures.[36] This probably represents a Christian interpretation of events, integrating an interrogation by the Sanhedrin with Mark's major theological concerns. Donahue concludes "the Markan narrative of Jesus before the Sanhedrin must be by-passed as a primary source for historical reconstruction."[37] Mark develops the trial as a synthesis of his themes: messiahship, discipleship, suffering, opposition to the temple, and the sonship of Jesus. The scene culminates in the High Priest's question "Are you the Messiah, the Son of the Blessed One?" (14:61), to which Jesus replies "I am," thereby turning the trial into "an epiphany of the Lord to the worshipping community."[38] Immediately, however, Jesus adds to this claim of divinity the dimension of the figure of the Son of Man, understood in Jewish tradition as the eschatological agent of redemption, but in Jesus' teaching the suffering servant too. This triple claim, Messiah, Son of God, Son of Man, precipitates the anger of Caiphas and the condemnation of the Sanhedrin: "They all concurred in the verdict 'guilty,' with its sentence of death" (14:64). Jesus is then mocked by members of the Sanhedrin and its officers (14:65).

While the Sanhedrin meets, Peter is in the courtyard. Although he had protested his loyalty at the last supper, Peter publicly rejects Jesus, ironically claiming "I do not even know the man you are talking about!" (14:71). Rejection is total: "the fishers of men" (1:17), "his companions whom he would send to preach the good news" (3:14), "the Twelve" (3:16), those to whom "the mystery of the reign of God has been confided" (4:11), those who have seen his power, witnessed the miracles, heard his teaching, testified to his Father's confirming voice, these disciples have all deserted him and fled.

Alone and abandoned, Jesus is taken to Pilate. The focus now changes from messianic claims to kingship, since the blasphemy associated with the former was not a crime punishable by death.

The title "king," not used prior to chapter fifteen, now appears several times (15:2, 9, 12, 18, 26), always with political overtones. Jesus remains silent before the accusations of the chief priests and Pilate.

The interrogation is followed by the story of the choice of Barabbas instead of Jesus for a festival release, a custom unknown outside of the gospels' reference. The crowds who had often supported Jesus now turn against him, and he is left forsaken by the world. The scene ends in ignominy and mockery, as disinterested and jeering soldiers ironically acclaim the true nature of Jesus' kingship.

Abandoned in death.   The description of the final stage of crucifixion also shows clear signs of Mark's editing, even though he may be using an already formulated crucifixion story circulated in the early Church.[39] Forsaken, rejected, betrayed, mocked, and scourged, Jesus is led to Golgotha. Since his self-acclaim before the High Priest (14:62-63), Jesus has remained silent before the overwhelming rejection by the world. "The passion story clearly becomes Mark's most eloquent statement concerning the person and mission of Jesus."[40] Alone he journeys to death, refusing even to drug his pain (15:23). When the procession arrives at the execution place, Mark impassively says "Then they crucified him" (15:24). Just another criminal to the soldiers, in fact another pretender who made their job more difficult (15:26), they leave him hanging there while they divide his clothes (15:24). The disciples who had fought for a place at his side in his kingdom (10:37) are nowhere to be seen, and the places they had wanted are taken by two criminals (15:27; 10:37).

The scene at the foot of the cross is a concentrated Markan christological statement. Thoughtless crowds mock Jesus' suggestion of the end of the temple, precisely at the time when its use becomes outdated; they call upon Jesus to save himself, while the reader knows his unwillingness to do so is salvific for all; they say a miracle will let them see who Jesus is, and "once again 'seeing' is tied to separation of Jesus from his cross."[41]

Alone in pain, the Markan Jesus has no comfort from friends, followers, beloved disciples, or mother. He is even rejected by his fellow prisoners (15:32). This is a time of darkness not only for Jesus, but also for the world, a darkness like the curse on the obdurate Pharoah (Exodus 10:21). Without exercising any control

(Lk 23:46) or revealing any sense of victory (Jn 19:30), the Markan Jesus expresses the feeling of being abandoned even by God (15:34), and "uttering a loud cry, breathed his last" (15:37). The end of Jesus' career is also its climax. An unknown centurion is the only person in the whole gospel to identify the Son of God with the crucified and abandoned man (15:39). What Peter and the disciples never understood was the true nature of Jesus' messiahship. The centurion gives us the only confession of the gospel—faith in the suffering Christ: "Clearly this man was the Son of God!" (15:39).

For Mark, Jesus' death is redemptive: "He saved others" (15:31), and it also provides a model for individual disciples and Christian communities such as Mark's to follow. Suffering and glory belong to different epochs, but triumph comes through suffering. The rejection and humiliation that Jesus experiences show his love, compassion, and dedicated servanthood. Thus Jesus fulfills scripture's many references to the Just One, relives the passion of David, and experiences the sufferings of the psalmist.[42]

Mark insists on the divine necessity of the passion (14:36) and shows Jesus' foreknowledge of it (8:31; 9:31; 10:32-34) and its cosmic effects (15:33, 38). At the same time he holds the Jews, Pilate, and the Romans morally responsible (14:64; 15:15). Moreover, the passion is as much a portrayal of the failure of discipleship as it is of Jesus' sufferings, and Mark clearly believes the crisis will only be overcome by faith in the cross and by life styles in conformity with that of the one who suffered.

Jesus—The Son of God

"This is my Son, my beloved."   Mark's suffering Jesus, who dies abandoned by the world, does not reappear to his disciples as he does in the other gospels. Although resurrection is implied (16:7), and has been prophesied (8:31; 9:31; 10:34), the actual ending of the gospel focuses on bewilderment and fear (16:8). In Matthew and Luke the glorious vindication of Jesus through his resurrection leads the disciples to worship him (Mt 28:17; Lk 24:52) and gives occasion for Jesus' solemn and authoritative commissioning of his Church (Mt 28:19-20; Lk 24:45-49). What is implicit in Matthew and Luke becomes explicit in John: "These have been recorded to help you believe that Jesus is the Messiah, the

Son of God, so that through this faith you may have life in his
name" (Jn 20:31). Mark contains no account of the resurrection
even though the story of the empty tomb suggests it; rather, the
principal focus remains the crucifixion. We must, therefore, look
elsewhere for Mark's presentation of the glory of Jesus and indications of his conviction that the suffering Jesus is also Son of God.

Mark begins his gospel with the clear statement that Jesus is
the Son of God (1:1) and follows this with one of two uses of
"Lord" meaning God in Isaiah's prophecy that refers to making
ready "the way of the Lord" (1:3). He presents Jesus as the one
who "comes" (1:9, 14, 24, 38), aware that he is sent by God (9:37)
and will return to him in glory (14:62). Jesus' supernatural origin
is revealed in his powerful words and deeds and the reaction of
the crowds expressing awe and amazement.[43] "What Jesus says
discloses his understanding of himself and his purposes. What
Jesus does reveals primarily the extent and nature of his authority
from God."[44]

In addition to his awesome ministry Jesus is directly acclaimed
as Son of God. Although the title is never used of Jesus by any of
his disciples, demons reverence him in this way (1:24; 3:11; 5:7),
and Jesus uses the title of himself (12:6; 13:32); it is used by the
High Priest (14:61), by the centurion at the foot of the cross
(15:39), and by God himself (1:11; 9:7). Moreover, the title Son of
God is used at other important points in the Markan narrative:
the title of the work (1:1), the ritual designation at baptism (1:11),
the transfiguration (9:7), the culminating moment of the trial
(14:61-62), and the confession at the cross (15:39). Two uses of "I
am" complement these references to Son of God: 13:6 can be
seen as an explicit messianic formula, and 6:50, being part of a theophany, could also have the deeper meaning of the divine title.[45]

The transfiguration is a scene of special recognition (9:2-8).
Paralleling the baptism, it contains the reality of the resurrection
and anticipates the Second Coming. It manifests the glorious
nature of Jesus as Son, attested to not only by Moses and Elijah,
but also by the voice of God himself.[46] Although Mark immediately
reminds his readers that they must interpret this theophany in
light of the suffering Son of Man (9:9), this scene is the true
centerpoint of Mark's gospel, the revelation of Jesus' glorious
and transcendent Sonship (1:1; 9:7; 15:39).[47]

What is announced at the beginning of the gospel and witnessed
at the transfiguration is ironically confirmed by the High Priest,

who links Jesus' messiahship with his sonship (14:61). Again Jesus will add the title Son of Man to the other two (Messiah, Son of God), confirming his understanding of messiahship as attained through suffering. However, throughout the gospel, Mark maintains that Jesus is the Son of God.

The Son of Man. The title which Jesus consistently uses of himself is "Son of Man." Although never used of Jesus by anyone else, it is the title that he uses to express understanding of his own mission.

In the Old Testament the title was used by Ezekiel to avoid self-designation, and is generally seen as an expression of humility. It is also found in the psalms (8:4; 80:16), but without eschatological meaning, and in the apocryphal book of Enoch, where it is linked to the messiah-king (1 Enoch 69:27-29; 70:1-2; 71:17). However, it is especially the references and imagery of Daniel, chapter 7:13-14, that form the Old Testament foundation for Mark's usage. Although Daniel refers to a human figure ascending to heaven to be confirmed in power, Daniel's figure and imagery gradually developed in pre-Christian apocalyptic tradition; it was interpreted first as Israel, and later as a pre-existent divine agent of redemption and as eschatological judge.[48] However, while this title is used occasionally in Jewish writings, here it is transformed, taking on originality as Jesus uses it in Mark's account.

Mark uses the designation Son of Man 14 times. Only two of these precede Peter's partial confession (8:27-33) and indicate Jesus' claim to forgive sin (2:10) and to be Lord of the Sabbath (2:28). Five uses come after the conclusion of the journey (10:52): two referring to the eschatological figure from Daniel (13:26; 14:62), and three referring to Jesus' betrayal (14:21[x 2] 41). Seven of the uses are contained in the journey section which, as we have seen, "functions as the central interpretive section of the Gospel."[49] In fact, Son of Man is a title that interprets all others. Although having authority to forgive sin, being Lord of the Sabbath, rising from the dead, and returning in glory, "the Son of Man has not come to be served but to serve — to give his life in ransom for the many" (10:45). Nine of the uses are in the context of suffering (8:31; 9:9, 12, 31; 10:33, 45; 14:21 [x 2], 41) and describe humiliation and rejection similar to that described in the tradition of the Suffering Servant in Isaiah (Isaiah 42:1-4;

49:1-6; 50:4-9; 52:13-53:12) or in the Book of Wisdom (Wisdom 2:10-20; 5:1-4).

While suffering is central to the concept of Son of Man, power and glory are too. In fact, the titles Son of Man and Son of God are functionally very similar. The Son of Man forgives sin, has authority over the Sabbath, rises from the dead, and comes in the glory of the Father accompanied by the holy angels, with great power and glory. He assembles his chosen ones from all over the earth, initiates the last drama of world history, vindicates his ministry, and presides as eschatological judge.

All the references to the Son of Man are linked to Jesus' authority[50] and emphasize his relationship to God. The Son of Man who suffers is clearly identified as a figure of cosmic power, and is implicitly linked to the Son of God in Jesus' response to the High Priest (14:61). If Son of God is Mark's climactic designation of Jesus, then Son of Man, another title of power, clarifies in typically Markan fashion the suffering component of sonship. In fact, it is the very rejection of the power and authority of the Son of Man which causes his suffering and eventual death.

Mark's portrait of Jesus is a paradox of life and death, power and helplessness, humanity and divinity. Jesus' origins are simple, his emotions strong, his need to pray evident. His ministry both reveals who he is and hides this knowledge from others. Mark sees Jesus especially as the great teacher who teaches with power and authority. This evangelist of suffering shows us Jesus in his pain, anguish, and death, but also in his sonship of power and glory. Only the disciple who can integrate faith in both the man of suffering and the Son of God can make the confession to which Mark's Jesus calls him: "Truly this servant on the cross is the Son of God" (15:39).

Chapter Five
DISCIPLESHIP IN MARK

"If a man wishes to come after me, he must deny his very self, take up his cross, and follow in my steps. Whoever would preserve his life will lose it, but whoever loses his life for my sake and the gospel's will preserve it." (8:34-35)

The gospel according to Mark is the work of a creative author and courageous pastoral leader who responds to the needs of the Church with a new and daring synthesis of the life and teachings of Jesus. While there is debate regarding the overriding purpose of Mark's gospel, there is substantial agreement among commentators that a clarification of the nature of discipleship was an essential part of the motivation behind this work.

Every chapter in the gospel of Mark has some reference to disciples or discipleship; the central section from 8:22 to 10:52 is a treatise on discipleship; all the people presented in the gospel are defined in terms of their relationship to the disciples; the portrait of Jesus is itself at the service of discipleship; this gospel's approach to the passion and deliberate omission of the resurrection appearances brings significant insights to the nature of discipleship; and finally, many commentators see the persecution of Christians in Rome as the pastoral need that caused Mark to write his gospel as a call to discipleship.

Mark's gospel is written with two main focuses on discipleship. He looks to the history and roots of Christianity and details the call and role of the disciples of Jesus. But he also focuses on the spiritual needs of Christians of his own time and challenges them to an appreciation of the nature of discipleship in their day. Through the utilization of the skills of the writers and dramatists of his time, Mark maintains this dual focus on discipleship so consistently throughout his gospel that it is viewed by some as providing the key to the interpretation of the whole work.

The Nature of Discipleship

The call of the disciples. Large crowds follow Jesus during his ministry and at times seem to anticipate the Church (1:27-28; 2:2; 3:7, 20, 32; 4:1; 5:21; 6:34; 7:37; 8:1; 10:1; 11:9; 12:37). However, Mark identifies a smaller number who are characterized by their faith, an awareness of the coming of the kingdom, and a commitment to follow Jesus. Sometimes these faithful and committed followers are referred to by name: Simon, Andrew, Peter, James, and John, Levi, Judas, Joseph of Arimathea, Mary, and Mary Magdalen; sometimes they are unnamed followers such as a centurion, some women, or people in the crowd. From the larger group of followers, the Twelve are singled out as those who truly hear the words of Jesus (4:1-34), witness his mighty deeds (4:35-5:43), and eventually participate in his ministry. Even among the Twelve, there are three, Peter, James, and John, who are called to a privileged position of attending to Jesus' teaching, witnessing special moments in his life (9:2-8; 14:32-42) and having personal access to Jesus' thought on important issues (9:9-13; 11:20-25).

Mark presents a special relationship between Jesus and his disciples: they are truly his (2:23) and are always with him (3:32-34). Jesus takes initiative in personally calling them (3:13-14) and establishes a fellowship with them that makes them his new family (3:31-35). With this group of disciples Jesus shares special experiences and teachings (10:33-34; 11:20-25; 14:12-26, 32-42).

In the first half of his gospel, before Peter's major confession at Caesarea Philippi (8:29), Mark describes four call scenes: those of Simon and Andrew (1:16-18), James and John (1:19-20), Levi (2:13-14), and the Twelve (3:13-19 and 6:7-13). These are complemented later with the general call of discipleship (8:34-38). These call scenes show that for Mark it is Jesus who takes the initiative in personally calling people to himself. His call implies a personal and unique response that includes commitment, obedience, witness, and mission. Those called leave family, job, and security without asking how or why. Their response is immediate, involves a total change of lifestyle and a willingness to suffer.

Disciples grow in their appreciation of their own life and mission as a result of their closeness to Jesus and develop a deeper understanding of the Lord's call to suffering. Their mission is not only a personal commitment to the Lord but also dedication to the fellowship they experience among themselves. They are called to prepare the new community (1:17) and sustain it in peace and perseverance (9:50). In this, they continue the ministry of Jesus who endows them with his authority (6:7-11), calls them to serve in his name (6:37-44), and permits them to mediate for him (9:14).

The disciples are his witnesses, trained and instructed by the Lord (7:17-23; 8:31). They are privileged to spend time with him (6:30-32), to see his glory (9:2-8), to receive his personal guidance (4:10, 34; 9:30-32; 10:23, 33; 11:20-25), and they are further assured of his continued presence (14:22-26).

Moreover, they are promised that in their commitment they will be sustained by the Lord who gives them knowledge of the secrets of the Kingdom (4:11), teaches them to pray (11:20-25), assures them of his presence (14:22-26), and guarantees them a reward (10:29-30).

The disciples—a puzzling aspect of the portrait. Mark presents the call and role of the disciples in very positive terms. However, he also presents them as lacking in understanding, fearful, under the sway of Satan, and even as the embodiment of opposition to Jesus. Moreover, their attitudes do not improve as the ministry progresses, but actually grow worse and end in desertion of Jesus in his moment of greatest need (14:50).

The disciples are portrayed as having a chronic inability to understand the essential revelation and message of Jesus. After the parable of the sower and seed, the disciples ask Jesus for an explanation, and he replies: "You do not understand this parable? How then are you going to understand other figures like it?" (4:13). After the espisode of the feeding of the five thousand, Mark comments "They had not understood about the loaves. On the contrary, their minds were completely closed to the meaning of the events" (6:52). When Jesus confronts the Pharisees with their hypocritical interpretations of the traditions of the elders, he says to the disciples: "Are you, too, incapable of understanding?" (7:18). When the disciples and Jesus were in a boat after the feeding of the four thousand, Jesus felt the need to say: "Do you still not see or comprehend? Are your minds completely blinded? Have you eyes but no sight? Ears but no hearing?" (8:17-18). The disciples' lack of understanding was particularly noticeable regarding the true nature of Jesus' ministry. They misunderstood the feeding stories (6:45-52; 8:14-21), the transfiguration (9:2-13), the Messiahship of Jesus (8:31-33), and particularly the doctrine of the cross (8:34-38; 9:31-37; 10:32-45).

Although they are privileged to be with Jesus and experience his power, the disciples are dominated by a paralysing fear, which seems to be an expression of their habitual misunderstanding. After Jesus calmed the storm, the disciples were afraid, and Jesus challenged them: "Why are you lacking in faith?" (4:40). When three of the disciples witness the transfiguration, they are struck with fear (9:6), and later when Jesus complements the transfiguration with foreknowledge of the passion the disciples "failed to understand his words, [but] they were afraid to question him" (9:32). They begin the final journey to Jerusalem in fear (10:32), a fear that eventually leads to flight (14:50). In fact, the gospel ends on a note of bewilderment and fear (16:8).

In addition to their fear and lack of understanding, the disciples throughout display attitudes of selfishness that result from temptation. When Peter rejects a suffering Messiah, Jesus reprimands him: "Get out of my sight, you Satan!" (8:33). Later, the disciples argue among themselves regarding rank and position (9:34) and try to monopolize and control other people's ministry (9:38). Even after being rebuked by Jesus, the sons of Zebedee again try to gain special privileges and position (10:35-45) and thus arouse the indignation of the ten (10:41). Toward the end of Jesus' ministry, in a moment when he needs support, the disciples fail the test and in weakness fall asleep (14:37). When the guards arrive, the disciples flee (14:50), and even though Peter returns, he ends by denying his Lord (14:66-72).

The disciples' unreliablility is a puzzling aspect of Mark's portrait. Although Jesus gives them special instructions, they fail to understand. Although Jesus sustains them, they are fearful. Although he speaks of suffering, they speak of power, and whereas he gives himself in service, they seek position and privilege. Their familiarity with Jesus is no guarantee that they will understand him. At times, the disciples seem to embody opposition to Jesus' teaching, or at least, represent a view of Jesus that Mark finds unacceptable for disciples in his own time.

The nature of discipleship in Mark. Mark's major teaching on discipleship, given on the way to Jerusalem, is bracketed by two stories of Jesus healing the blind (8:22-26; 10:46-52). In the first story of the blind man at Bethsaida, Jesus heals him in two stages: first he sees only dimly, then after a second stage of healing, he sees perfectly. In the second story of blind Bartimaeus, the healing is immediate and total because of his faith, and after the cure, Bartimaeus "started to follow him"—an image of discipleship.

What Jesus does for these two blind men describes exactly what he is doing in this section of the gospel for those who wish to be his disciples: he is opening their eyes to appreciate who he is. The first blind man sees a little—just as Peter sees Jesus as Messiah (8:29). However, everything is not clear at first, and it will take further healing before Peter sees that the Messiah must also suffer (8:31-33).

When Mark describes the disciples of Jesus, he does so with an eye on Christians of his own day. As disciples of Mark's day read this story, they can appreciate both the greatness of the disciples of Jesus and their essential weakness in grasping the importance of the cross. Almost every episode of misunderstanding, fear, and temptation relates to a misconception of the nature of Jesus' messiahship as a life of service and suffering. As Mark's fellow Christians read this good news in the light of their own call to follow the Lord, they are constantly challenged to ask themselves whether they are doing any better than Jesus' disciples did. Can they see fully, or is further healing still needed before they will see the Lord as he is?

Discipleship involves a close relationship with Jesus (4:34; 9:2-8). Disciples are called by Jesus, taught by him, and follow him. They are called to appreciate both his transfiguration and glory (8:27-30; 9:2-8) and his cross (8:31-33; 9:30-32). They are called to become the new family of the Lord (3:31-35). This centrality of Jesus is based on a relationship of faith. The recognition of who Jesus is brings peace (4:39-40), healing (2:5; 5:34), and effective ministry (9:14-29).

Discipleship involves not only a relationship between Jesus and his followers, but it also implies a relationship among the disciples. Jesus relates to them as a community and challenges any of their attitudes that disrupt their life together (9:33-37; 10:35-45). The communion, fellowship, and witness value of their life as a community seems to be part of the essence of their call (1:17).

Discipleship is also a call to mission and ministry. It implies detachment from family and occupation and a commitment to courageously preach the teachings of Jesus to all (8:35-38). In fact, discipleship is a call to sacrifice one's life for Jesus for the sake of the gospel (8:35).

Above all, in Mark, discipleship is a fellowship in service, suffering, and death. This is the major focus of Mark, both in his evaluation of the disciples of Jesus and in his challenging of his own. Even when speaking of the rewards of discipleship, Mark adds that they will come "with suffering" (10:29-30). Suffering is an essential part of Jesus' life, and he promises his disciples it will be part of theirs too (8:31-38; 9:35-37; 10:42-45). In fact, the only true disciple is the person who appreciates the need of suffering as part of one's commitment to imitate the Lord. Even though Mark knows of Jesus' resurrection (16:6), no appearances are given. Thus the focus remains on the suffering and death.

In Mark, discipleship results from the call and healing illumination of Jesus. It consists in a personal relationship with Jesus and with other believers. It also leads to mission, ministry, and the upbuilding of the community. It is above all a fellowship in service and suffering.

Requirements for Discipleship

Faith. Disciples are called personally by Jesus to follow him. No explanations are given them, but their response is immediate and implies detachment from relatives, possessions, and one's own way of life. Just as Jesus' messiahship in Mark is seen more in his deeds than in his discourses, so also the nature of response in faith is seen more in actions and relationships than in statements on faith itself.

However, on a few occasions, Jesus does explicitly comment on faith. He criticizes the chief priests, scribes, and elders for not having put their faith in John the Baptist (11:31), condemns anyone who scandalizes the simple faith of others (9:42), and warns disciples against putting their faith in false messiahs (13:21). Mark's clearest criticism of false faith is his condemnation of any linkage between faith and a Christ removed from the cross (15:32).

Jesus is thrilled when he sees the faith of the paralytic's friends (2:5), but saddened by the weak faith of the disciples (4:40), the crowds (9:19), and his own townspeople (6:5-6). On other occasions he urges individuals (9:23) and his disciples to faith in the power of God (11:22-24).

In Mark the disciples are called to believe in the power of Jesus and appreciate its origin (4:40-41; 6:50-52; 11:21-26). Acknowledging that power, they are then called to faith in Jesus' way of suffering (15:30-32, 39). For those who believe in the power that authenticates his teaching and in the necessity of the cross, "Discipleship is the only form in which faith can exist."[1] In discipleship, faith is demonstrated in "an unashamed association and identification with Jesus," and in "a persevering fidelity and commitment to his words and mission."[2] The former calls for a progressive recognition of Jesus, his ministry of selfless service, his self-gift in suffering, and the disciples' compelling need to be least, to be servants, and to lose their lives for others. The challenge to fidelity in faithful mission is highlighted through a series of stages of growth in faith, developing from call, election, and mission, to service, following, and sharing in the passover.[3] Above all, the disciples' faith focuses on a sharing in the suffering servanthood of Jesus (8:34-38; 10:23-31, 46-52).

Mark is as much interested in engaging the faith of his readers as he is in narrating the life of faith of the original disciples. This faith is not so much based on Jesus' teachings as it is on his deeds. For Mark, discipleship is another way to present his christology.

Understanding. In the last section we saw that the disciples' chronic inability to understand Jesus is a puzzling dimension of Mark's portrait of them. He seems to use them to portray attitudes unacceptable for disciples, an approach not used by Luke. However, "their failures constitute the primary literary device by which the narrator reveals Jesus' standards for discipleship, for much of his teaching comes in the course of correcting their behavior and attitudes."[4] As the disciples move from lack of understanding to misunderstanding, and eventually to failure, Jesus intensifies his private instructions, and Mark challenges his readers to develop a correct understanding of the Lord. "This movement indicates that the failure of the disciples is a deliberate literary and theological construction of the evangelist."[5] Mark is stressing that familiarity with Jesus as his close associate does not assure a correct understanding of him. Time and again the disciples do not think the way Jesus thinks (8:33), nor appreciate the prime values of his ministry (10:38). They are amazed at his miracles (1:21-28; 5:35-43; 7:31-37), but do not draw the necessary conclusions of faith. Their misunderstanding, highlighted from chapter four to chapter eight, is complemented by their fear before Jesus' healings (5:1-20), his transfiguration (9:2-8), his power over nature (4:35-41), and his resurrection (16:1-8). This fear leads to denial, flight, and final abandonment of the Lord.

The disciples' astonishment at the miraculous power of Jesus is due to their misunderstanding of its true source (6:52), and the fear they manifest at his control over nature (4:41) and before the theophany of the transfiguration is likewise the result of misunderstanding (9:6); fear limits the effectiveness of their ministry (5:15) and their ability to appreciate the importance of the journey to Jerusalem (10:32).

In the garden, the disciples' misunderstanding is again stressed as an explanation of their failure (14:40). Even denial is associated with misunderstanding, as Peter ironically acknowledges that he does not know Jesus (14:68, 71).

We have already seen that Mark considers understanding so central to authentic discipleship that he brackets the journey to Jerusalem—his central section on discipleship—with the two healings of blindness, the first in two stages, indicative of the disciples need for further enlightemment to dispel their partial blindness.

Mark is concerned with the needs of his own community and its new catechumens. When the disciples misunderstand, Jesus instructs; when they are afraid, he supports them and gives them courage; when they fail to see the link between sonship and suffering, he refocuses their attention on it. In fact, "Only by understanding what the disciples failed to understand can the catechumen he initiated into the mystery of Christ."[6] The increasing failure of the disciples to understand is a Markan technique that warns the members of his community of their own possible failures and challenges them to return to an authentic understanding of Jesus and his call to them.

Prayer. The Markan Jesus is "absorbed in prayer" at critical points in his own ministry: at the beginning, after the first miracles (1:35), after the feeding of the five thousand who had gathered to receive him in the wilderness (6:46), and in Gethsemane as he prepares for the sacrifice ahead (14:32-42). On each occasion he prays alone, at night, recommitting himself to his

Father. His prayer exemplifies faithfulness for disciples in their own fear and uncertainty.

Jesus teaches that the disciples' prayer is intimately connected with faith and action. In 11:24, he equates prayer and faith, and in 12:40, condemns the emptiness of prayer without service of others. Although Jesus had given the Twelve power over evil spirits (6:7), and seemingly they had exorcized in his name (6:30), nevertheless on at least one occasion they were unsuccessful in driving out the mute spirit from a possessed boy (9:17-18). Jesus indicates that their powerlessness is the result of weak faith (9:19), and later in private adds "This kind you can drive out only by prayer" (9:29). Thus he again links faith, prayer, and effective ministry: disciples must not rely on themselves, but rather on the power of God.

Jesus urges disciples to pray for what they need with confidence (11:24), insists that the final trials will be bearable (13:18), and urges them to be vigilant and pray for grace to withstand temptation (14:38).

Jesus' last days in Jerusalem are the occasion for a major teaching on prayer (11:22-25). This Markan collection of Jesus' sayings, found scattered in the other synoptics, becomes the main synthesis of Jesus' teaching on the qualities of the disciples' prayer. It must be permeated with confidence in God (11:22), deep faith (11:23), and trust in Jesus' words (11:24). To these qualities is added one requiring the disciples to he reconciled among themselves before coming before the Lord (11:25); a condition probably added to Mark's original text under the influence of the frequent liturgical recitation of the Our Father (Mt 6:14).[7] This collection of teachings presents the basic challenges of the Our Father, which is otherwise not found in Mark. For a community undergoing persecution, the Our Father must not be merely recited, but rather must be embodied in concrete attitudes of faith and discipleship.[8]

Community.   Although several individuals respond to Jesus with one or another quality appropriate to disciples (5:18, 22-43; 10:46-52; 15:39, 42-46), the primary inner group are personally called by Jesus (1:16-20; 3:13-19) and established "as his companions" (3:14), a community that spends its time "in his company" (1:20). In Mark, Jesus is rarely seen alone, but generally accompanied by his followers. They may fail him, but they are always

"the men he himself had decided on" (3:13). They are privileged
to be constantly with him, instructed, commissioned, and
prepared for the mission ahead (4:11-12, 33-34; 6:7-13, 37-43;
9:30-31).

This community of disciples is at times the historical Twelve,
and at times Mark's own Church. Called to obey the will of God,
these disciples become the new family of Jesus (3:31-35). They
have a new relationship with each other as a result of their new
relationship with Jesus. Mark gives few ethical rules, and those
he presents generally focus on relationships within the community: the permanence of commitment between husband and
wife (10:2-12), the acceptance of children (10:13-16), the need to
share one's wealth (10:17-25), and the centrality of mutual love
(12:28-31).

If Jesus' teaching on the community dimension of discipleship
is directed to Mark's community, then it is because that community is experiencing bitter conflict. "Misunderstanding,
dissension, and even betrayal reside with the Christian community itself."[9] To such disciples Jesus addresses a brief collection of teachings, sometimes referred to as the discipleship
discourse (9:33-50). These instructions are given privately to the
disciples, "inside the house" in Capernaum (9:33). This group of
sayings is stitched together with catchwords: "in my name"
(9:37, 38, 39, 41), "little ones" (9:37, 42), "cause to sin" (9:42, 43,
45, 47), "Gehenna" (9:44, 46, 47), "fire" (9:44, 48, 49), "salt"
(9:49, 50).[10]

These instructions on community challenge the disciples to
reject ambition (9:33-37) and stifle their own desire to control
the membership of the community (9:38-41). They urge attitudes
of service and acceptance of even unimportant members. Finally,
they warn against scandal (9:42-48) and false security in one's
own commitment (9:49-50).

Thus a community component is integral to discipleship in
Mark. It means forming a new family for Jesus, being dedicated
to servant attitudes, and being aware that membership is not a
guarantee of fidelity.

Discipleship as Union in Suffering

A life of detachment. The dedication of the disciple to Jesus
must be total. Every dimension of life must be integrated in one

great thrust of self-gift to the Lord, and nothing must weaken or detach one from this total self-commitment. Anyone who wants to preserve his or her life, be first, and share the Lord's glory, must reject worldly priorities for life, serve all, and share the Lord's cup of suffering.

The disciples respond to Jesus' call by leaving everything that can deter them from a singlehearted commitment to follow him: Simon and Andrew "immediately abandoned their nets and became his followers" (1:18), and James and John "abandoned their father Zebedee" (1:20). When Jesus sent out the Twelve to minister in his name, "He instructed them to take nothing on the journey but a walking stick—no food, no traveling bag, not a coin in the purses in their belts" (6:8), and they were told "Do not bring a second tunic" (6:9).

Although the Twelve often fell short of Jesus' expectations, Peter could say "We have put aside everything to follow you!" (10:28). Mark here uses an aorist tense, implying a once-and-for-all decision to leave everything, and then uses a perfect tense to signal the enduring nature of that decision.[11]

Disciples are called to be detached not only from their material possessions (1:16-20) and occupations (3:13-14; 10:50),[12] but also from the pursuit of wealth (10:20-25), the desire for rank and privilege (9:35; 10:37-38), the support of family (10:29), and from the desire to be actively involved in ministry with Jesus (5:19). Although placed in positions of leadership over the community, the Twelve must be detached from all desire to control and dominate (9:38-42), from previous misunderstandings of the meaning of messiahship (8:31-33), from the teachings of their former religious leaders (12:38-40), from the security of institutions (13:1-2), from prior rituals (2:18-20), from former interpretations of the Law (2:23-28), and even from religious experiences (9:2-8). The episode of the rich young man reminds disciples that they must be detached not only from wealth but also from "a piety of achievement."[13]

Jesus' demands are rigorous in comparison with those of his day. Judaism saw wealth as a blessing, and the scribes prohibited giving away everything, precisely because it reduced a person to poverty, but Jesus still insists "Go and sell what you have and give to the poor" (10:21).[14] Judaism also legislated against adultery, but in ways that excluded a husband's infidelity to his wife. Jesus' directives are again more rigorous while at the same time

protecting the wife's rights too. This code of conduct would also
be seen as a rigorous sexual ethic by the Roman Gentiles in
Mark's community.[15]

Jesus calls for renunciation of all that is detrimental to a
single-minded commitment to him. This new life, based upon
relationship with Jesus and his disciples, is a hard road to follow
(10:23-24), for it leads to Jerusalem (10:52). During the journey
Jesus addresses himself nine times to any person who would be
willing to follow him: "If a man wishes to come after me. . . .Who-
ever would preserve his life. . . .If anyone wishes to rank first. . .
whoever welcomes me. . . .Anyone who is not against us. . . .Any
man who gives you a drink of water. . ." (8:34, 35, 38; 9:35, 37
[x2], 40, 41; 10:43). These appeals to surrender one's life totally
to Jesus make concrete the detachment, self-denial, and cross-
bearing, required of those who want to be disciples of the Lord.

Selfless service of others.   From their very first encounter,
Jesus tells those whom he calls that they will become "fishers of
men" (1:17). When he decides on the Twelve, we are again
reminded that he will send them to preach the good news (3:14)
and give them authority to exorcize (6:7). The only time the
disciples or the Twelve are designated "apostles" (6:30) is after
they return from ministering in his name. However, it is clear
throughout that the inner core of disciples are called to share
Jesus' mission and authority. We have seen that the detachment
to which disciples are called must include detachment from position, status, control over others, power, and privilege. The
disciples' union with Jesus must include imitation of his selfless
service of others: "The Son of Man has not come to be served but
to serve—to give his life in ransom for the many" (10:45). The
disciples' responsibility not only includes ministering in the
name of Jesus, but ministering in the way Jesus ministered.

The discipleship discourse (9:33-50) again provides the occasion to focus ministry on selfless service. In response to the
disciples' argument "about who was the most important" (9:34),
Jesus says, "If anyone wishes to rank first, he must remain the
last one of all and the servant of all" (9:35). He then reinforces
his teaching by focusing the disciples and their concern for importance on a child whom Jesus sets in their midst. Since the
Aramaic word for child and servant is the same, this child stand-
ing in the midst of the disciples is a symbolic portrayal of what

ought to be the disciples' attitudes as they minister in Jesus' name: humility, trust, helplessness, dependence, awareness that they have no rights, and service.[16]

The disciples' selfless service is their key ministerial quality. People will not be brought to Jesus through the power and persuasion of the disciples' authority and importance, but through the simple attitudes of childlike service: "Whoever welcomes a child such as this for my sake welcomes me" (9:37).

This teaching on selfless service, powerful though it is, does not register well with the disciples; James and John still yearn for privilege and special positions in the kingdom. Jesus responds by comparing leadership in his Church to other forms of leadership and the exercise of authority. "You know how among the Gentiles those who seem to exercise authority lord it over them; their great ones make their importance felt. It cannot be like that with you" (10:42-43). Calling the disciples to reject this world's values, Jesus challenges them to reverse the relationship between being served and serving. Authority figures in Jesus' Church, who are definitely set over others, do not achieve their ministry through domination but through service. "Anyone among you who aspires to greatness must serve the rest; whoever wants to rank first among you must serve the needs of all" (10:43-44). This selfless service will include detachment from success in ministry. "If any place will not receive you or hear you, shake its dust from your feet in testimony against them as you leave" (6:11).

Being united with Jesus in his suffering implies a life of detachment and selfless service. As John the Baptist anticipated Jesus' suffering servanthood (1:7), so the disciples will prolong it (8:35; 9:35; 10:43-45).

Sufferings of the community. The disciples' response to Jesus' call was immediate, a fact that inspires disciples of all times. Yet, throughout this gospel, one has the nagging feeling that their following of Jesus was not without self-interest. They wanted glory for their leader (8:29, 32), a share in it for themselves (9:5), rewards for their dedication (10:28-31), as well as rank and privileges (9:34; 10:35-37). When they shared Jesus' power they rejoiced (6:30), but when they were ineffective they were disturbed (9:28). Each time Jesus challenged them to realize that suffering was part of his life and theirs too, they rejected his message (8:31; 9:31; 10:33-34)—they always seem to be judging by human standards and not by God's (8:33). When James and John accept the cup of suffering, they do so as a step to the special positions they seek (10:35-39). Jesus struggles to help the disciples see the need of suffering as part of their discipleship. "But when Jesus began to talk about rejection and death, the disciples evidenced how much they had expected glory and power."[17] Although during the journey they had been formed by the Lord to realize the importance of suffering (8:22-10:52), shared the Lord's cup (14:23), and pledged their willingness to die (14:31), they quickly forget their commitment (14:37-38) and refuse all suffering (14:50). "Jesus loses his life and thereby saves it, while the disciples try to save their lives but lose."[18] They are as totally disinterested in the suffering dimension of Jesus' messiahship as they are in the suffering dimension of their own discipleship. Mark's fleeing young man and sleeping disciples ironically portray failed commitment.[19]

By means of his treatment of the disciples' failure, Mark again centers the reader's attention on a teaching crucial to faith—that suffering is essential to discipleship.

Mark's call to his community to integrate the acceptance of suffering into their Christian dedication permeates the narrative. He draws the reader into an appreciation of the meaning of suffering in Jesus' life, constructs the central section of his narrative as a journey towards an appreciation of the importance of suffering, and portrays Jesus, the Son of Man and Suffering Servant, as the model of suffering discipleship. He ends by pointing out that the disciples were absent from the burial of Jesus, and by suggesting that no one who rejected the sufferings of Jesus was around for his resurrection.

In spite of the disciples' blindness, Jesus' teaching is very clear. "If a man wishes to come after me, he must deny his very self, take up his cross, and follow in my steps" (8:34). Once the journey ends in the place of suffering, Jesus presents his farewell address in which "the connection between the passion of Jesus and the passion of the community is made."[20] Jesus informs the disciples they too must anticipate suffering as he does. "They will hand you over to the courts. You will be beaten. . . .You will be arraigned . . . men [will] take you off into custody. . . . Brother will hand over brother for execution . . .children will turn against their parents and have them put to death . . .you will be hated by everyone" (13:9-13).

Discipleship is a union in suffering. Disciples experience it in the daily detachments that commitment to Jesus requires. They live it in their ministry of selfless service. They anticipate it in the carrying of the crosses that make up life and result from living as Jesus did.

Discipleship in Times of Uncertainty

Examples of fidelity. Jesus sends his disciples, especially the Twelve, to preach the good news (3:14), exorcise in his name (6:7), teach (6:30), testify to their faith (13:9), and proclaim the good news to all nations (13:10). We have already seen Mark's frequent negative approach to the Twelve as he criticizes their misunderstanding of Jesus' life and teaching, their seeking after glory, and their rejection of the Lord. However, the disciples' failures are never deliberate, but always the result of weakness. This portrayal of infidelity shocks the reader in Mark's community into a realization of what can happen, even to the best. It is a daring way to focus on the need of fidelity and the ever-present danger of infidelity. Hearing the words of Jesus, seeing his miracles, and witnessing his glory is no guarantee of fidelity.

In Mark's community, as the modern reader knows, the leading disciples eventually become models of fidelity, spreading the message throughout the world, and dying for their faith. In Mark's narrative, however, they are "Not examples by which their own worth or failure is shown, but examples through whom teaching is given to the community and the love and power of God made known."[21] Writers like Matthew and Luke show how the disciples, and especially the Twelve, embody the teachings of Jesus by documenting their faithfulness and leadership of the community.[22] Mark calls his community to appreciate the importance of fidelity by dramatically showing the scandalous consequences for the community of recognizing infidelity in its leaders. Readers of this gospel may find themselves criticizing the disciples, reversing their decisions, and establishing criteria for fidelity in Church leaders.

Mark's portrait of the disciples highlights three qualities of fidelity, two positive and one negative. First, the disciples are always in the company of Jesus; this is the most important element of discipleship. Second, Jesus is always faithful, no matter how revolting the disciples' infidelity becomes, an assuring characteristic for a community anticipating persecution, as Mark's may have been. Third, their evident weakness becomes a challenging way to arouse indignation in the readers, enabling them to focus on the essential need of fidelity in Church leaders who are not only "fishers of men" but must faithfully exemplify the teachings of the Lord, as models for their communities.

Equality in discipleship.   Disciples become Jesus' new family: "These are my mother and my brothers. Whoever does the will of God is brother and sister and mother to me" (3:34-35). Not only are they family to him, but also to each other (10:30). This new family is made up of "insiders" to whom Jesus reveals everything, and they contrast with the "outsiders" to whom everything is a riddle (4:11). The outsiders "will look intently and not see, listen carefully and not understand" (4:12). The outsiders are the scribes, Jesus' fellow townspeople, his family—in fact, all those who should know him best. At times the disciples themselves have some of the characteristics of outsiders and are accused of the same failures: "Have you eyes but no sight? Ears but no hearing?" (8:18). However, in general, the disciples are among the insiders.

The new family of Jesus centers on the Twelve, but consists of many others as well. "For Mark the Twelve and the disciples are not necessarily the same group."[23] Moreover, disciples are a part of the crowd which itself "serves to complement the disciples in a composite portrait of the followers of Jesus."[24] The final group Mark refers to is the women from Galilee who follow Jesus. None of these are sub-groups, and none are an inner elite with more power and privilege than the others. They each have strengths and weaknesses. If historically the Twelve, or the three—Peter, James, and John—have special status, Mark's presentation clearly rejects this concept, for "there can be no suggestion of an inner elite among them; if ever such existed it is now abolished."[25]

Discipleship is not the privileged possession of a restricted group. "Anyone who is not against us is with us" (9:40). Jesus was indignant when disciples kept the children away from him (10:14), and he affirmed the ministry of an unnamed healer who showed confidence in the power of Jesus' name (9:39), ironically pointing out that the healer would not speak ill of him, even though the disciples would.

Several individuals are very positively portrayed by Mark: Peter's mother-in-law (1:31), the confident leper (1:40, 45), the friends of the paralytic (2:3-5), Jairus (5:21-23), the woman with a hemorrhage (5:25-34), the Syro-Phoenician woman (7:25-30), the father of a possessed boy (9:24), Bartimaeus (10:46-52), the poor widow (12:41-44), the woman who anointed Jesus (14:3-9), and Joseph of Arimathea (15:42-46). These minor characters, "the little people," "consistently exemplify the values of the rule of God. . . . their anonymity in no way diminishes their importance. . . .Taken collectively, their impact on the reader is unmistakable and profound."[26] When contrasted with better-known disciples, they exemplify Jesus' teaching that the least will be first (9:35).

Mark presents many followers, none of whom seem to embody all the qualities of discipleship; each seems to have an equal call and an equal opportunity to respond or to minister.

Women. Luke is the evangelist who gives most attention to women, but perhaps Mark is the one whose focus on women is both surprising and most enlightening. Coming fifteen to twenty years before the Lucan refinements, Mark gives us a first glimpse of early Christianity's break with male-dominated Judaism.

Some commentators think Mark presented faithful women as alternatives to the faithless Twelve,[27] or as a strong power base in early Christianity,[28] or as models of discipleship.[29] Others find these views too optimistic and see Mark's approach to women as very similar to his approach to men: they are neither ignored, nor put on pedestals, they "supplement and complement the Markan portrayal of the disciples, together forming, as it were, a composite portrait of the fallible followers of Jesus."[30] Mark's treatment of women is a further indication of equality in discipleship.

Jesus never uses examples of women in his teachings or parables. However, he works miracles for two women: the woman with the hemorrhage (5:25-34) and the Syro-Phoenician woman (7:24-30), and at men's request, cures two other women: Simon's mother-in-law (1:29-31) and Jairus' daughter (5:21-24, 35-43).

When Mark mentions women he highlights qualities of discipleship that they exemplify: Simon's mother-in-law's spirit of service, the hemorrhaging woman's faith, the Syro-Phoenician's boldness and confidence, the widow's generosity (12:41-44), the unknown woman's compassion (14:3-9), the faithfulness of the women who went to Calvary (15:40-41, 47) and their care for their dead Lord (16:1).

Mark also underlines the roles of women in the way he structures or locates episodes describing them. The healings of women balance those of men.[31] The poor widow demonstrates authentic dedication (12:41-44), in contrast to the hypocrisy of the temple's religious leaders (12:38-40). The unknown woman's anointing of Jesus is bracketed by the plotting of the chief priests (14:1-2) and the betrayal by Judas (14:10-11). She "gives up money for Jesus and enters the house to honor him (14:3-9), and Judas, the man who gives up Jesus for money. . . leaves the house to betray him (14:10-11)."[32] The entire passion narrative begins and ends with stories of women's compassion for Jesus (14:3-9; 16:1-8).

The ending of Mark stresses the women's fidelity in contrast to the men's desertion of Jesus. Although the women flee the tomb, bewildered and in fear, they are nevertheless the only ones to witness the empty tomb and be told of the resurrection (16:1-8).

Mark portrays women in their strengths: service, faith, boldness, confidence, and witnessing. However, he also shows us the doubting of Mary, his mother (3:21, 31-32), the immorality and violence of Herodias (6:19-29), the fear and disobedience of the women at the tomb (16:8). Mark's portrait reemphasizes the universality and equality of discipleship: it is "both open-ended and demanding; followership is neither exclusive nor easy."[33]

Prophetical witness. Disciples were called to courageously proclaim their dedication to Jesus (8:38) and be a lamp on a stand for all to see (4:21). Left in charge until the master returns, they were to be vigilant in looking after his interests (13:32-37) and promote the realization of the kingdom.

Mark's is not a handbook of directives for ministry, rather he tells the story of Jesus and the implications for prophetical witnessing emerge. For example, the readers who are disciples see Jesus overcoming evil and know that they are called to overcome the power of sin in their own communities. As Jesus lives in tension with the evil of his world and challenges the injustices of society and religion in the controversy stories, so his disciples must be on their guard, live in tension with the world's values and proclaim the good news. Persecution, expected in times of uncertainty, gives opportunity for witnessing to the word even to the Gentiles (13:10).

Disciples' prophetic witness is directed by the Holy Spirit, and so they are told "do not worry beforehand about what to say. In that hour, say what you are inspired to say. It will not be yourselves speaking but the Holy Spirit" (13:11).

Their responsibilities will include vigilance to insure correct teaching, and care lest the community be led astray by false messiahs and false prophets (13:22). This vigilance includes sensitivity to the signs of the times (13:28-29).

Above all, the prophetic witness of disciples will be the courageous living and proclaiming to others of the necessity of accepting suffering as a way of acknowledging the Son of Man. When others seek comfort and the miraculous, disciples call for suffering servanthood.

Mark's teaching on discipleship is at first puzzling, but eventually there emerges for the reader perhaps the most radical call to follow the Lord of any evangelist.

Chapter Six
THE KINGDOM OF GOD

*"Let the children come to me and do not hinder
them. It is to just such as these that the kingdom of
God belongs. I assure you that whoever does not accept the reign of God like a little child shall not take
part in it." (10:14-15)*

Mark's community lived in times of uncertainty, crisis, and persecution. Distant both geographically and culturally from the Palestinian origins of the gospel, the community struggled to make
Jesus' eschatological message alive in their times and relevant
for their circumstances. They believed Jesus had brought a new
period of history and confided his message to them. The challenge
produced not only a need for personal conversion but also for
communal conversion, and it is to the latter that we turn in this
chapter.

Jesus preached the arrival of the kingdom, but established it
on the foundation of his community of disciples. The community,
with strengths and weaknesses, is referred to as Jesus' family,
house, boat, flock, and temple. The community has simple structures, focusing primarily on sharing life in the Lord. It is a community under threat as it faces crises on its pilgrimage to God.
Finally, it is a ministering community, dedicated to prolonging
the mission of Jesus in outreach to the world.

The Kingdom of God

Nature of the kingdom. Divine kingship was a common concept in religions of the middle-east, and in most cases the earthly
ruler was viewed as a representative of the god-king. In the time
of Israel's judges, when each nation had its own god, Yahweh was
understood as the king of Israel (Judges 8:23). The prophet
Samuel was reluctant to allow this divine kingship to be shared

with an earthly monarch (1 Samuel 8:6), but eventually he yielded
to the people's insistence (1 Samuel 8:19-22). Israel then believed
that the kings of Israel were appointed by Yahweh (1 Samuel
10:24; 16:12; 2 Samuel 7:12-16), shared his sovereignty (2
Chronicles 13:8), and were his sons (2 Samuel 7:14).

Beginning with Elijah, Israel's concept of divine-kingship
took on broader dimensions, and by the time of the great prophets, Yahweh's sovereignty was seen to be universal; all nations
were subject to him (Amos 1-2), his kingdom was everlasting, and
he ruled over all creation (Isaiah 52:7; Psalms 103:19; 145:13).

Prophetical teachings on God's powerful rule through a kingly
and consecrated nation (Exodus 19:6) had to be reconciled with
Israel's defeats by, first, the Assyrians and then by the Babylo-
nians. This was done by interpreting God's rule as universal but
future (Isaiah 2:2-4), to be attained through an eschatological
kingly figure (Isaiah 9:6-7; 11:1-9; Micah 4:1-4).

The Synoptic gospels frequently mention "the kingdom of
God" or "the kingdom of heaven", phrases that refer to God's
reign or rule rather than a localized kingdom. Mark uses the concept "kingdom [or reign] of God" fourteen times. It is a sug-
gestive image, and "a metaphor for God's power manifest in the
life and teachings of Jesus."[1] More than an image or metaphor,
"kingdom of God" is a symbol: that is, it is an image that evokes
appropriate attitudes and suggests specific responses.[2] The arrival of the kingdom requires reform of life and faith in the
gospel (1:15). The understanding of the nature of the kingdom is
reserved only to the disciples (4:11). It does not result in a spectacular political conquest, but is a hidden and small seed that
quietly grows by itself and becomes a place of refuge for all (4:26,
30). Jesus understood the kingdom as future, but its arrival as
imminent (9:1). He taught that those wishing to enter into God's
kingdom must sacrifice all that might impede their entrance
(9:47). Life in the kingdom is not earned but given to the childlike
(10:14-15). It is hard to enter the kingdom (10:24), especially for
the wealthy who are attached to their possessions (10:23, 25).
Those who appreciate the centrality of love and wholehearted
dedication to God are close to the kingdom (12:34). The establishment of the kingdom, to which the devout look forward (15:43),
is linked to the death of Jesus (14:25).

Mark considers that the eschatological kingdom, longed for in
the Old Testament, is established with the coming of Jesus, the

Son of Man, of whom Daniel said: He received dominion, glory, and kingship; nations and peoples of every language serve him. (Daniel 7:14). The kingdom is communal, made up of a new people of God (4:11; Daniel 7:27), and is established through conflict with the kingdom of Satan. Paradoxically, Israel's failure to accept Jesus leads to an inability to recognize the kingdom's arrival.

The inauguration of the kingdom. The Markan Jesus' inaugural message is "The reign of God is at hand!" (1:15). The only speech in the Galilean ministry deals with the reserved membership in the kingdom (4:1-34). Mark synthesizes the requirements for entrance into the kingdom (10:13-31) and indicates that with the destruction of the temple the place of God's reign must be found elsewhere (11:12-26; 13; 15:37-38). "In effect, we see Mark writing a history of the Kingdom, and he does so in order to assign to his own people a place of hope in the midst of it."[3]

In a story that recalls the first creation when the Spirit hovered over the waters, Mark affirms that the kingdom comes with Jesus who receives the outpouring of the Spirit as the prophets had foretold (Isaiah 11:2; 42:1; 61:1-2), specifically indicated by his appearance in the form of a dove, an ancient symbol of kingly designation.[4] Jesus then goes into the wilderness, the place of covenant (Exodus 34:28; 1 Kings 19:8), where the overthrow of Satan's rule begins (1:12-13).

After John's arrest, Jesus announces that "the reign of God is at hand" (1:14-15). Some commentators, favoring a realized eschatology, understand Jesus to claim that the kingdom is already here. Others, focusing on 9:1, see this passage (1:14-15) as referring to the imminent realization of the kingdom. The life and ministry of Jesus is the basis for proclaiming a new era, attained in fullness at his death (9:1; 14:25), but anticipated in the power of his ministry (1:15).

As Jesus journeys throughout Galilee, he proclaims the arrival of the kingdom. His controversies with the Pharisees show the dimension of mercy that the reign of God brings (2:1-3:35). His healings and exorcisms demonstrate the destruction of the reign of Satan (3:23-27), and the superiority of Jesus' rule. His parables challenge all to appreciate the gratuitous nature of the kingdom, to accept its call, and to realize that the kingdom is not made up only of the perfect, but also of those who live in tension, undergo conversion, and respond in various degrees (4:1-25).

When Jesus arrives in Jerusalem, Mark portrays the crowds as saying: "Blessed is he who comes in the name of the Lord! . . . Blessed is the reign of our father David to come!" (11:9-10). Thus, Jesus' first appearance in Galilee announces the arrival of the kingdom, as does his first appearance in Jerusalem; both anticipate his final return in glory (14:62).

Following Jesus' entrance into Jerusalem, Mark presents the end of the temple's function as a central place of encounter with God (11:12-26), the end of the chief priests' religious authority (11:27-33), and heralds the rebuilding of a new place of worship.[5] Mark's anti-temple motif climaxes when "the curtain in the sanctuary was torn in two from top to bottom" (15:38). The kingdom, realized in its fullness at the death of Jesus, is realized apart from the temple and Judaism. "Jesus proclaimed that the new deliverance was incapable of being incorporated into the old framework."[6] Rather, the kingdom is now open to the sinners not the self-righteous (2:17), and to a few chosen ones (4:11), who make up the new family of Jesus (3:31-35).

Although Mark does not use the word "Church," the kingdom is made up of the disciples who gather around Jesus. Signs of the kingdom's presence are offered to Jews and Gentiles, whose following of Jesus and obedience to the will of God make them insiders to whom the mystery of the kingdom is now confided.

Discourse on the kingdom.   The most detailed characterization of the kingdom is provided in the parable discourse (4:1-34). This is the largest section of Mark devoted to Jesus' teaching on the kingdom, and is both a window through which we can look at Jesus' understanding of the kingdom, and also a mirror in which we see ourselves and examine our own attitudes to the kingdom.[7]

The parable of the *sower* (4:1-20), which is the interpretative key to all the other parables (4:13),[8] presents four responses to the word of invitation to the kingdom. It expresses the mysterious nature of human responses to the kingdom (4:11); some accept and others reject. "The nature of the Kingdom is such that it provokes antagonism, dividing the audience into insiders who can perceive and outsiders who cannot."[9] Some of those to whom the invitation is made do not have the strength to withstand the onslaught of the kingdom of Satan (3:23-27; 4:15). Others, having accepted the word, weaken under the pressures of persecution (4:17), and still others receive the word but produce no fruit because they are not singleheartedly dedicated to the kingdom, but are attached to wealth and this world's values (4:18-19). Those to whom the kingdom is confided are not uniform in their dedication but produce varied degrees of fruitfulness (4:20).

At this point in the discourse Mark introduces a collection of sayings found scattered in Matthew and Luke. Mark has compiled them in a distinctive way and related them directly to the context of parables on the kingdom.[10] Mark understands the lamp to be Jesus himself in whom the kingdom is present. The mystery of the kingdom, confided to those who receive the word, is that Jesus embodies the kingdom and "there will come a day when . . . He will be known as the Bearer of the Kingdom in a disclosure which all will see."[11] There follows an urgent appeal to listen carefully to the proclamation of the kingdom (4:23). One's present attentive response determines future reward. The measure of one's present dedication will determine final reception into the kingdom. "Only those who penetrate the mystery in the present will share in the glory which is yet to be revealed. Because God enters the world through the word of the Kingdom proclaimed by Jesus, the matter of one's response to Jesus is of ultimate seriousness."[12]

The parable of the sower, scattering the word of invitation to the kingdom, explains human responses to the word. Human acceptance or rejection because of weakness, rootlessness, or attachment, determines membership in the kingdom. However, there is another side to the word scattered like seed; it has a power of its own, and grows effortlessly. For those who respond to the word of invitation to the kingdom the proclamation of Jesus takes root in their hearts, grows, and matures, until it is ready for harvest (4:26-29). This exclusively Markan parable, in emphasizing divine initiative and the efficacy of the word proclaimed, complements the human dimensions of success and failure as seen in the *sower* parable.

Mark proceeds to describe the kingdom in terms of what happens to the mustard seed (4:30-32). Although small when sown, its future is great. The kingdom's beginnings may be hidden (4:22), its message even initially reserved for a small group of insiders (4:11-12), but eventually it will be openly revealed, have remarkable growth, and be amazingly productive (4:32).

This Galilean discourse summarizes Jesus' distinctive understanding of the kingdom, gives insight into its nature, and focuses on the current needs of Mark's community.

The Christian Community

Disciples as a community. Mark frequently presents the disciples as lacking in faith, misunderstanding the message, and abandoning Jesus. Nevertheless, Mark sees the disciples, and especially the Twelve, as a core group that forms a new community around Jesus. They are always with him as his companions (3:14). Gathered around him (3:32, 34), they are the insiders who receive special instructions (4:11). As a group they follow Jesus throughout Galilee and up to Jerusalem. They express their dedication to him by leaving their former lives and publicly sharing their faith (8:29). From the beginning, Mark always presents Jesus and the disciples together as a community. Jesus and his mission are seen in light of the group's formation and future, and even their abandonment of Jesus is seen in relation to their pledged sharing (14:22-31). In spite of their many weaknesses, the disciples are the new community, the foundation of the kingdom, and the original gathering of the Church.

Mark's understanding of Church is expressed through simple images. His concerns about misguided leadership, status seeking, and false structures lead to a reserved ecclesiological synthesis.

The Christian community, the kingdom of God's people, is the new family of the Lord (3:31-35). Faith in Jesus and obedience to the Father's will are the criteria for membership. Earthly family ties are no longer important (6:4), but through faith and obedience anyone can enter the eschatological family of the Lord. Although brothers and sisters to Jesus, the disciples must live in view of the family union that comes at the end of time. Jesus does not return to the community after the resurrection, but like the bridegroom (2:19) is physically absent from his Church.

The gathering of disciples around Jesus frequently takes place in a house that serves as a place of withdrawal, opportunity for special instruction, retreat from the pressures of ministry, and occasion to be together with brothers and sisters in faith. Mark's frequent references to a house recall the households of the Lord, or house-churches of early Christianity;[13] and provide the historical basis for a possible practice and understanding in Mark's community.

A third image of the Church which Mark finds in his sources but also introduces into his own editorial passages is that of the boat.[14] Jesus proclaims his message from the boat (3:9; 4:1), the disciples gather with Jesus in the boat, and experience the manifestations of his power and are challenged to increase their faith (4:35-41; 6:47-52). In the boat Jesus provides special instruction to his disciples (4:10-12; 8:14-21).

On two occasions (6:34; 14:27) the followers gathered to hear the message of Jesus are referred to as the flock of God. The first is in the context of the feeding of the 5000 in the wilderness that recalls the exodus and the covenant, and the second precedes the death of Jesus: "I will strike the shepherd and the sheep will be dispersed" (14:27). "In each case the inter-relation between the leader and the group is explicitly stated."[15] Jesus is the shepherd and the community of his followers are the flock.

A fifth Markan image of the Church is temple, used twice during the passion. The Christian community is the new temple of God, "not made by human hands," which replaces the old temple and becomes the basis for the kingdom of God (14:58; 15:29).[16]

Requirements for life in the community.   We have already examined the requirements for personal commitment to Jesus and seen the disciple's need for faith, understanding, prayer, community, and the acceptance of suffering. Here we consider the specific requirements that follow from the challenge to live as the new people of God.

The disciples' repentance and faith result in a radical break with their previous ways of life and the setting up of a new life together in community. The Twelve, the core of a new community, come from varied backgrounds, experiences, and regions. This group is expanded to admit others, including Gentiles, a tax collector, women, the sick, and the possessed. The ecumenical nature of the community contrasts with the exclusiveness of the Jewish sects, like the Pharisees and the Essenes, and demands new attitudes of acceptance of others who wished to approach Jesus through the community (10:13-14).

The disciples form a community of mutual service, in which each member, with childlike openness, lives as the least and the servant of all (9:33-37). The community must rejoice in the spread of the name of the Lord, and not develop into a closed group like those that were so common in the Judaism of Jesus' time (9:38-40).

Mutual service and mutual appreciation require the removal of all scandal within the group (9:42). This demands active practice of self-control (9:43-48) and the acceptance of passive purification from God (9:49).

Mark has little interest in casuistry, and the absence of ethical material from his book shows he did not think his community needed it. Only 10:2-12 seems like a part of an ethical code of conduct for the community. Jesus reverses Moses' decree and rigorously condemns divorce.

The Jews saw wealth as a blessing, but Jesus requires a spirit of poverty and sharing from his followers (10:21-22). The world of Jesus' day saw prestige and status as important, but Jesus requires a spirit of selfless service of others (10:35-45). The Jews opposed Rome, and many, such as the Zealots, formed revolutionary groups, but Jesus requires a just relationship to the state and accepts the need to pay just taxes (12:13-17).

Repentance, faith, openness to all, mutual service, and childlike trust characterize the community. It rejoices in good wherever it appears, avoids scandal through ascetical practices, gives increased value to marriage, shares with the poor, and lives in dialogue with the state.

Sharing in the community.   Jesus' new community is not maintained by common prescriptions and laws, whether ethical or ritual. There are few of the former, and indications that Jesus rejected the latter (7:19). Mark's community may face outside persecution and internal differences regarding authority and christology. However, apart from the apostles' envious response to James' and John's ambition (10:41), there are no indications of division, no appeals for reconciliation, other than the brief reference in 11:25, and no prayers for unity.

Mark's community prays together (11:17, 22-25), undergoes religious purification (9:43-50), fasts (2:18-20), values almsgiving (12:41-44), shares with the poor (10:21), and collaborates in Jesus' redemptive mission (3:14; 6:7). Mark's main teaching on the sharing within the Christian community comes in his feeding stories, and we now consider these.

Several meals are mentioned at which Jesus is present: Levi's meal for his tax-collector friends (2:15-17), the feeding of the 5000 (6:34-44), the feeding of the 4000 (8:1-10), and the Last Supper (14:12-26). To these can be added a general comment by the Pharisees on the way the disciples take their meals without the prescribed ritual washing (7:2). Each of these meals is an occasion for significant teaching, but the two feedings are of particular importance. Since their language, situation, and content are so similar, the two feedings could be doublet accounts of the same tradition. However, Mark carefully integrates them into two cycles of stories and produces significantly different insights. Each feeding concludes a cycle of miracle stories[17] and is followed by an episode on the sea of Galilee, conflict with the Pharisees, controversy over bread, a healing, and concludes with a confession of faith.[18] The structure and framing of each cycle shows Mark's deliberate intention to reinterpret them as two different incidents.

The two stories reflect the constituencies of the early Church and stress the value of table-fellowship because of faith in Jesus. He prays to his Father and commands the people to gather into table-groupings. The crowds are very large, when one remembers that Capernaum and Bethsaida had populations of about 2000-3000 each. The first feeding is of 5000 Galilean Jews. Five loaves are used to feed them, possibly symbolic of the five books of the Pentateuch, and twelve baskets are left, possibly symbolizing the twelve tribes. The second feeding is of 4000 Gentiles in the Decapolis. Seven loaves are used, possibly symbolic of the seventy nations into which the Jews divided the world. Seven baskets are left over, possibly symbolizing the seven Hellenistic deacons of Acts. The two stories portray the providential care of God who in Jesus calls the people to fellowship, and offers to all, whether Jew or Gentile, the same blessings and food of Jesus' presence.

Both feedings are in the wilderness and precede a crossing of the Sea of Galilee. The people are grouped in the same way Moses arranged his followers in the wilderness (Exodus 18:21). The context recalls the exodus and there are indications that even the crowds saw the gathering as a basis for a messianic uprising.[19] These feedings show the community's awareness that they are the new exodus people of God, sharing together their pilgrimage to the kingdom. Rejecting false messianism, Jesus refocuses attention on his way of suffering.

The sharing of fellowship and of the covenant in the wilderness is complemented with the eucharistic sharing of the Last Supper (14:22-25). Even in the feedings, the apostles shared the bread of Jesus with the crowds of followers. Here, anticipating his departure (14:25), Jesus institutes the sacrament of his continued presence—a meal of fellowship, union, and eschatological hope.

Moreover, it is also a participation in sacrificial self-gift (14:24). Whether the Supper is a passover meal is not certain. However, Mark's general framework clearly recalls the Passover (14:12-16) and speaks of redemption and liberation (14:24). The community, called to share in this self-gift (10:38), is challenged to put the miraculous feedings into the context of the suffering and death of their Lord, for "eating with Jesus includes an emphasis upon his death, resurrection, and absence."[20]

Mark's community shares a variety of ascetical practices. It also shares the richness of Jewish-Gentile membership, lives together a new exodus, shares table-fellowship, the eucharist, and a communal participation in the sufferings of the Lord.

Authority in the Community

God's commandments and human traditions.   When the Pharisees criticize Jesus' disciples for not observing the prescribed ritual washing before eating, Jesus calls them hypocrites and quotes the strong condemnation of Isaiah: "This people pays me lip service but their heart is far from me. Empty is the reverence they do me because they teach as dogmas mere human precepts" (7:6-7; Isaiah 29:13). Jesus then adds: "You disregard God's commandment and cling to what is human tradition" (7:8). This attitude of Jesus to laws established by men is evident from the early times of his Galilean ministry. Leprosy is a skin disease that also caused ritual impurity and made the person a social outcast (Leviticus 13:45-14:57). When a leper requests a cure, Jesus disregards all the accumulated laws governing interaction with lepers, and he "stretched out his hand, touched him, and said: 'I do will it. Be cured' " (1:41). Jesus violates the cultic ritual prescriptions of Moses in favor of compassion.

In a major confrontation with the Pharisees who condemn the disciples' plucking of grain on the Sabbath, Jesus lays aside their scrupulous legal interpretations and bluntly affirms: "The sabbath was made for man, not man for the sabbath" (2:27). This teaching is then exemplified in Jesus' public and deliberate rejection of pharisaic Sabbath laws, when he cures a man with a withered hand on the Sabbath (3:1-6). Jesus "looked around at them with anger" (3:5) and cured the man. The Pharisees were so provoked by this compassionate miracle that they "began to plot with the Herodians how they might destroy him" (3:6).

The woman with a hemorrhage is another outcast (5:25-34), being in constant ritual impurity. Her touching Jesus would have rendered him unclean according to the Pharisees. However, he does not seem disturbed at all by the woman's condition; on the contrary, he praises her faith.

Jesus changes Mosaic teachings to refocus his disciples' attention on the priority of God's mercy. But when dealing with the detailed additional prescriptions of the elders and pharisaic leaders his rejection is even stronger. He condemns their practice of korban, whereby goods dedicated to God could not be used to help others, saying, "you nullify God's word in favor of the traditions you have handed on" (7:13). Moreover, korban is not the only practice he condemns. "And you have many other such practices besides" (7:13). The episode concludes with the abrogation of all the ritual food laws of Judaism. "Thus did he render all foods clean" (7:14-23).

Jesus' approach to authority and to various detailed laws and prescriptions is a constant challenge for religious leaders of all times. Laws introduced to defend faith and practices developed to manifest faith frequently end up being more emphasized than the faith itself. This is as evident today as in Jesus' time, and his compassionate outlook is as clearly needed.

Structures in the community. Jesus declares "Whoever does the will of God is brother and sister and mother to me" (3:35). Elsewhere he affirms "Anyone who is not against us is with us" (9:40). Several episodes present disciples other than the Twelve as serving the Lord (1:31), proclaiming the power of Jesus (1:45; 5:19; 7:36), exorcising in his name (9:38-39), following him (10:52), witnessing the empty tomb (16:5-6), and being commissioned to proclaim the resurrection (16:7).

We have seen the negative portrait of the Twelve and the fact that they are not formally reinstated after their denial and abandonment of Jesus. They receive no final commission as in Matthew and no outpouring of the Spirit as in Luke and John. Nor does Jesus return in his post-resurrection power to authenticate their authority as he does in the other Synoptics.

In studying the ecclesiological structures in Mark some writers consider that Mark's emphasis is principally on the unstructured local house-churches.[21] Others see his negative assessment of the Twelve and the Three as an indication of his rejection of the authority structures of the Mother-Church in Jerusalem.[22] Trocmé thought this rejection had led Mark to become the spokesperson of a breakaway missionary movement among the common people of Palestine.[23]

While Mark rejects authority based on ritual, law, temple-institution, and family relationships, I remain unconvinced that Mark represents a Church structure that is a rival to that of the Twelve. He criticizes them, condemns them, and warns against their misunderstanding and weak faith, but the Twelve remain the central authority structure. The "Twelve," used without the qualifier "apostles," appears ten times in Mark, in comparison with six uses each in Matthew and Luke, four in John, and one each in Acts and Paul.[24] Jesus personally calls the Twelve (3:13), gives them authority to preach, exorcize (3:14-15; 6:7), and teach (6:30). Later, he commissions them to feed the people (6:37; 8:6).

In spite of their weaknesses, the Twelve remain the authoritative group. While Peter, James, and John are the privileged three, they are not given any more authority as an inner elite than the rest of the Twelve. The Twelve, trained and instructed by Jesus, are specifically warned regarding their style of authority, and challenged to practice a servant leadership (9:33-42; 10:35-45) and suffering selfless service of others (10:38).

Mark's is the first gospel, and he does not represent the more detailed structures evidenced in the Acts, or the more venerated position assigned to the apostles in "Q."[25] Mark gives us both the primitive structure of the Twelve and warnings regarding over-emphasizing this structure. Other gospels will fill out the picture, but the centrality of the Twelve is already present in Mark.

The leadership of Peter. The list of the Twelve is headed by Peter (3:17), who is the first to be called by the Lord (1:16). Previously referred to as Simon (1:16, 29, 30, 36), Jesus gives him the name "Peter," meaning "a rock." He is prominent among the Twelve, leading them (1:36), speaking for them (9:5; 13:3), questioning Jesus on their behalf (10:28), expressing their understanding of Jesus (8:29), and affirming their commitment to him (14:31).

Although privileged with several special experiences of Jesus, Peter is never the exclusive beneficiary. Even his so-called confession is really a confrontation with Jesus regarding the place of suffering for the Messiah (8:27-31). His dedication and loyalty are clear (1:16-18; 10:28; 14:31, 66), but as we have seen, so too is his weakness. Like the rest of the Twelve, he sleeps when the Lord needs him, abandons the Lord, and rejects him. Jesus ends by returning to Peter's original name, Simon (14:37).

Mark's portrait of Peter is frank but no more an attack on Peter than is any other New Testament writing.[26] The last time we see Peter he is sobbing at his denial of Jesus (14:72). These are the only tears shed in the gospel of Mark and suggest a genuine conversion for Peter. The last time we hear of Peter is when the young man at the tomb instructs the women to report to Peter (16:7), thereby hinting at a reinstatement, in spite of Peter's abandonment of the Lord.

Mark's portrait of Peter agrees with what we know of him from Paul. While the other gospels embellish the image of Peter, their similarity to Mark is clear. Peter is preeminent among the apostles, a leader, and spokesman. He vacillates and makes mistakes, but clearly he wants to be loyal and wants to succeed. Mark makes no explicit mention of any special authority for Peter, although his portrait is easily seen as the basis for the more authoritative presentations of Matthew and Luke.

A Community Under Threat

Crisis at hand.   Mark's is a gospel filled with suspense and conflict. The controversy stories (2:1-12, 15-17, 18-22, 23-28; 3:1-6) show Jesus dealing with problems of vital concern to Mark's community: forgiveness of sin, relationship with social and religious outcasts, the question of fasting, and Sabbath observance. As we have seen, Mark's frequent use of "be on your guard" warns his own community of crises ahead. The Markan Jesus complements his emphasis on the need for watchfulness by encouraging the community to be sensitive to the signs of the times (13:28-29).

Mark is not a handbook of ethical regulations or of discipline for the community, but a challenge to face the overwhelming problems of the day with the insight that comes from knowing the authentic Christ. It is a response to the crises at hand, whether from conflict with religious authorities or from changing world conditions.

Jesus is in conflict with the evil spirits, and he exorcizes them, with the Pharisees and experts in the Law, and he debates with them, with disciples and their misunderstanding, and he confronts them. The disciples receive their first warnings of temptation

and conflict in the parable of the sower. They will face crises provoked by Satan and his alluring kingdom, by persecution that
comes with faith in Jesus, and by attachment to this world's
wealth and values (4:13-20).

As the disciples' boat is tossed by the storm, they are reminded
of the crisis that results from weak faith that makes them incapable of facing the storms of life (4:35-41; 6:50-52). The crisis
of faith can result in denial and betrayal, even by close associates
of Jesus—a very strong warning to Mark's community.

Mark punctuates his gospel with crises and conflicts with
Jewish religious leaders. These episodes lack the bitterness of
Matthew's opposition and may indicate that the Christian's
separation from Judaism is still incomplete and not yet ir-
revocable. Nevertheless, the authorities' legalism, protection of
the status quo, overemphasis on institutions, and outmoded practices and rituals are positions that Mark feels he must confront.

Mark reformulates faith for a Church facing the crisis of expansion and cultural adaptation. No longer a small Jewish sect
restricted to Jerusalem, the Church is now expanding throughout
the known world. This calls for adaptation linked to fidelity to
the roots, and Mark, writing for his Roman Church, provides
both. In fact, writing a gospel is part of his response to crisis.

A farewell to a pilgrim people. The major summary of the
crises to be faced by the community is presented in the Jerusalem
discourse of chapter thirteen. This discourse complements the
parable discourse of chapter four, identifying both the crises to
be faced and the encouraging conviction that Jesus will ultimately
triumph. This discourse is the longest one given by Jesus; in fact
the only uninterrupted sermon attributed to the Lord by Mark.

Analyses of chapter thirteen "have shown that members of
Mark's church find their faith strained to the breaking point by
the insufferable conditions of their time."[27] As Daniel had written in response to the crises of life under Antiochus IV, so Mark,
himself influenced by Daniel, writes to challenge and encourage
his community, faced by surrounding darkness and dismay.
Several authors consider this discourse to be so central to Mark's
purpose that they see the whole gospel as an apocalyptic work.
Certainly they see chapter 13 as a Markan apocalypse modeled
on Daniel.[28] More recently, other writers see this as "a revision of
the apocalyptic traditions,"[29] or as "a farewell discourse of the

type found in Deuteronomy 32 and John 14-17."[30]

This discourse is given on the Mount of Olives, itself significant in Jewish tradition as the place of judgement and the glorious appearance of God.[31] It is addressed to Mark's community as its members face the crises occurring between the resurrection and the final return of the Lord. Some of them may well have been "caught up in a resurgence of apocalyptic expectation" occasioned by the Roman attack on Palestine, or by belief that after their forty years of trials they would enter the promised kingdom soon.[32] Certainly, they are confronting a major crisis that some feel could mark the end.

Having heard Jesus' prophecy of the end of the temple, the apostles ask: "Tell us, when will this occur? What will be the sign that all this is coming to an end?" (13:4). Jesus describes the initial troubles (13:5-13), the great tribulation (13:14-20), the rising of false messiahs (13:21-23), the coming of the Son of Man (13:24-31), and the need of constant vigilance (13:32-37).

Jesus refers to a series of problems that are already part of the crisis faced by Mark's community, beginning with "Be on your guard. Let no one mislead you" (13:5). False teachers and false understandings of Jesus are the first critical areas that need attention. False prophecy, false interpretations of Christ "will lead many astray" (13:6).

Jesus then speaks of war, "but this is not yet the end" (13:7), it is just part of the age of crisis. The Roman presence in the land does not signify the end of the age of waiting but is just one of the crises of life.

A major component of the critical conditions faced by Mark's community is persecution. In words reminiscent of his own sufferings, Jesus reminds them they will have to face persecution, arraignment, beatings, betrayal, hatred, and death. Persecutions will offer occasions to spread the message even to the Gentiles. In all these crises, "the man who holds out till the end is the one who will come through safe" (13:13).

Jesus now goes on to speak of a profanation so serious it will provoke the end of the temple and should be an indication to the Christians that the time has come to flee. The "abominable and destructive presence" originally referred to the statue of Zeus set up by Antiochus IV (Daniel 9:27), but it is not clear what Mark has in mind. It could be the statue of Caligula that the emperor intended setting up in the temple in the year 40, a plan prevented by his death. Since Mark uses a masculine participle with a neuter noun, he could have a specific historical person in mind, in which case the investiture of the fool Phanni as high priest in 67-68 could be viewed as the sacrilegious presence, or possibly Titus and his Roman standard, or his troops surrounding the city. It could also refer, less precisely, to the Anti-Christ. Mark tells his community that when they recognize this "abominable and destructive presence"—"let the reader take note!" (13:14), they should flee, for it will be a sign of awful trials ahead.

As frequently happens, times of external crises are accompanied by internal crisis for the community, as various individuals suggest various responses. False prophets, many of them undoubtedly believing they are guiding the Church correctly, "will appear performing signs and wonders to mislead, if it were possible, even the chosen" (13:22). Jesus repeats his earlier warning against false religious interpretations of his presence and message: "So be constantly on guard! I have told you about it beforehand" (13:23).

Moving from the community's immediate crises, Jesus turns to describe the cosmic drama of the triumphant return of the Son of Man to gather the chosen (13:24-31). The period of trial will end with the exaltation of the Son and the vindication of those who persevere through the crises that discipleship entails. Whatever the trials, Mark's community must live in anticipation of the Lord's triumph. Thus they must live with vigilance and sensitivity to the signs of the times (13:32-37).

A community of the end times. The farewell discourse often tells the disciples "Be on your guard," "take note," "be constantly on guard," read the signs of the times, see and appreciate, "stay awake!" Although the end has not come and the disciples must not yield to panic (13:7), nevertheless, they are challenged to live as pilgrims in anticipation of the end. Jesus affirms that the time of fulfillment comes with his message (1:15; 9:1), demonstrates its presence through exorcisms and miracles, and prophesies its glorious consummation (13:26; 14:25, 62). As we have already seen, the life and ministry of Jesus leads to the Church's period of waiting for the final return of the Lord. With Jesus' coming the eschatological age has dawned, and the crises of the present are "the onset of the pains of labor" (13:8) that gives birth to the final kingdom. As a community, Christians now live in the end times. The gospel's abrupt ending is a further reminder that we are in process, and must struggle to realize the hidden and mysterious reign of the Lord, for "things are hidden only to be revealed at a later time" (4:22).

As the community lives through crises, faces hardship and the sacrifice of possessions and wealth, and suffers persecution for the kingdom, its members are assured that they will "receive in this present age a hundred times as many homes, brothers and sisters, mothers, children and property—and persecution besides —and in the age to come, everlasting life" (10:30).

This period of end time expectation offers a time for conversion (1:15), for delight in the new wine of Jesus' message (2:22), for sharing in the new covenant (14:24), for dedicated acceptance of the cross (8:34), and for the gaining of life (8:35-36).

Mark's community sees Jesus as the agent of a new age and themselves "as an eschatological covenant people called into being by Jesus, the eschatological prophet, and charged by him to carry forward its mission in the world."[33]

They now vigilantly live in expectation of the Lord's return. "As to the exact day or hour, no one knows it, neither the angels in heaven nor even the Son, but only the Father" (13:32). That final act of deliverance will constitute their community as the kingdom of God. Although its beginnings are small and hidden, the community is quietly growing all the time (4:26-29), and before the end will be a home where all will find rest (4:30-32).

Mark urges his Christian community to face up to its crises, whether internal or external, to be sensitive to and appreciative of the awful problems that come to each age, and to live in watchfulness as they prepare for the Lord's return.

A Ministering Community

The mission of the Church. In the first scene depicting the call of the disciples, Jesus identifies their future mission: "I will make you fishers of men" (1:17). The story concludes that they "went off in his company" (1:20). This brief missionary program anticipates Mark's understanding of the mission. He does not give details of mission for the Church, rather those "he himself had decided on" (3:13), his disciples, "went off in his company" (1:20) "as his companions whom he would send to preach the good news" (3:14). Mark's focus is not on what they will do, but

that they are with him. "Being with Jesus qualified the Twelve
to bear witness to him and to participate in his distinctive ministry
of proclamation and the overthrow of demonic power.[34]

The choice of the Twelve and their mission to preach and exorcize (3:13-19) is linked chiastically with the apostolic mission in
which they are sent again to preach and exorcize (6:7-33).
Following the former (3:20-35) and preceding the latter (6:1-6)
are episodes of rejection. In the center of this parallel arrangement are the parables with their theology of proclamation (4:1-34)
and the miracles with their theology of exorism (4:35-5:43).[35]
Thus, the whole section, punctuated with the typically Markan
emphasis on rejection, is seen as structured on the mission of the
early disciples to preach and exorcize. It ends with the disciples'
return from their mission, and this is the only time Mark calls
them "apostles" (6:30). Apart from this brief experience of work
for others, the disciples' principal task is to remain in Jesus'
company.

As has already been noted, Mark's purpose is to challenge his
community to live their brief mission in spite of crisis. Eventually,
they are to bear witness (4:21-25), proclaim the word to the Gentiles (13:10), and make use of their talents for the benefit of the
kingdom (12:1-12).

Unlike the other Synoptics, Mark has no final solemn commission from Jesus to his Church. Mark has four endings: the canonical ending (16:9-20), composed in the second century, is a synthesis of ideas from Luke and John. It is not found in the best
manuscripts and is not Mark's work. The shorter ending consists
of three lines added after 16:8 to round off the abrupt ending. Its
vocabularly is clearly non-Markan, and the absence of reference
to it by the Fathers of the Church indicates its later origin. A
third ending is found in one manuscript preserved in the Freer
Gallery of Art in Washington, D.C. This ending, known to St.
Jerome, seems to have been written to soften and explain this
gospel's presentation of the apostles' hardness of heart. The
authentic Markan ending is 16:8.

The episode of the empty tomb, brief though it is, forms Mark's
final commission. The young man reminds the frightened women
that the person who has been raised is "the one who was crucified"
(16:6). This identification of glory and cricifixion is what the
disciples ought to have learned while in Jesus' company. The
young man again diverts the Church's attention away from glory

to suffering; this is not only the theology of Mark's entire work, it
is also the mission of the Church: to live and proclaim the suffering servanthood of Jesus. Throughout the time of Jesus' ministry,
the disciples flee from this faith, and the women at the tomb do
just the same; they "fled from the tomb bewildered and trembling; and because of their great fear, they said nothing to anyone"
(16:8). Mark wrote his gospel to provoke responses in his readers.
This ending is an invitation to his readers "to reflect on their own
response to the dilemma which the women faced."[36] Did Mark's
community adequately appreciate that the Son was also a suffering Lord? Were they bewildered and trembling at the implications of their faith? Were they silent? Or rather, regardless of
their fear, were they willing to share the Lord's mission to proclaim his message to all?

Outreach to the Gentiles.   Jesus first ministers in Galilee, a
region with many Gentile connections. He also travels to Gentile
areas: Gerasa, the Decapolis (5:1-20; 7:31-37), Tyre and Sidon
(7:24-30). Moreover, he works miracles in Gentile areas similar to
those he performs in Jewish areas (1:21-28; 5:1-20), and the people responded in faith (5:18-20; 7:29-30).

Mark is probably written for Gentiles. He explains Jewish
customs (7:3-4; 14:12; 15:42), diminishes the importance of the
Law (2:23-28; 7:14-23), shows that Jesus' message is accessible
to the Gentiles (7:27-30; 8:1-10; 13:10), and praises the Gentiles
(5:18-20; 7:29-30; 15:39). He frequently presents Jewish leaders
in a bad light, but not the Gentiles. Mark also presents his
theological convictions that the Lord will "turn his vineyard over
to others" (12:9), "the good news must first be proclaimed to all
the Gentiles" (13:10), the chosen will come "from the four winds,
from the farthest bounds of earth and sky" (13:27), and "the
good news is proclaimed throughout the world" (14:9).

Jesus' first trip across the lake to the Gentile area of Gerasa
produces the significant exorcism of Legion and the condemnation of the swine (5:1-20). The exorcism parallels Jesus' first exorcism for Jews (1:21-28), but this one ends by symbolizing the
exorcism of the Gentile lands, as the unclean swine leave the
land and are drowned. This miracle signals Jesus' intentions and
the future mission of the Church to the Gentiles. Unlike others
who are healed, the man in this episode is not silenced, but encouraged to proclaim what God has done (5:19).

Jesus' cure of the daughter of the Syro-Phoenician woman
(7:24-30) expands his ministry even more than his trip to Gerasa
did. Here he ministers in a new region, to a different nation, and to
a woman. Moreover, this passage presents the first Gentile believer.

The implications of Jesus' missionary activity are synthesized
in his rejection of food laws (7:15, 19) and his condemnation of
the temple authorities' money-changing practices that effectively
exclude Gentiles from the temple that should have been a house
of prayer for all nations (11:17).

Jesus' ministry takes place around the lake that separated
Jewish and Gentile lands. In Mark, the same lake becomes a symbol of the unity of Jews and Gentiles in the kingdom. "The boat
trips, alternating between the two sides and giving each side due
blessing and respect, dramatize a unitive movement."[37] What
Jesus does on one side of the lake for the Jews, he does on the
other for the Gentiles. Thus, for example, we have seen the feeding
of the 5000 in Jewish lands and the feeding of the 4000 in Gentile
regions. In the second feeding, Jesus has pity on the Gentiles after
three days—a possible reference to his death and resurrection.
Thus, "The beginning of the Gentile mission is projected into the
time after the death and resurrection."[38] Returning from this
second feeding, the disciples have one loaf with them in the boat
(8:14). Jesus questions them about leaven and bread, but they
misunderstand his implications. The one loaf becomes a symbol
of the unity of the Church that Jesus had been achieving through
his ministry to both Jews and Gentiles.

Jesus' ministry and his challenge to the disciples to appreciate
the unity of the future Church is complemented by Jesus' call for
a mission to the Gentiles (12:9-11; 13:10, 27; 14:9). The final statement at the tomb: "He is going ahead of you to Galilee" (16:7)
redirects the Church's attention to the Gentile features of that
first region in contrast to the exclusivism of Jerusalem. "It is a
reasonable claim that in Mark 14:28 and 16:7 'Galilee' has come
to symbolize the Christian mission to the whole world, not simply
Galilee in the literal geographical sense."[39]

Jesus' ministry ends in the unity of faith of the Gentile centurion (15:39) and the Jewish member of the Sanhedrin (15:43).

Ministering in Jesus' name. Jesus did not gather disciples
around him to study the Torah as the rabbis did with their disciples,

but he called them to send them out to preach (3:14). While companionship with Jesus is central to Mark's understanding of authentic discipleship,[40] it results in service to others.

Ministering in Jesus' name did not lead to the acquisition of power or status (9:33-37), but to the Church's selfless service modeled on that of Jesus (9:35-37; 10:42-45). "The Son of Man has not come to be served but to serve—to give his life in ransom for the many" (10:45). Jesus gave precise directives to his ministry teams as he sent them out to preach and exorcize: "take nothing on the journey but a walking stick—no food, no traveling bag, not a coin in the purses in their belts" (6:8). Nothing about them reflected wealth or status, but only poverty and simplicity. Elsewhere Jesus said: "Whoever welcomes a child such as this for my sake welcomes me" (9:37).

Ministering in Jesus' name brings responsibilities to the disciples.[41] They must be aware of their obligation to take care of others (6:37-39; 8:4-7), to collaborate without vying for power (9:33-37), and to share their ministry with others (9:38-41). Above all, anyone wishing to participate in Jesus' ministry must share his cup of suffering (10:38), take up his cross, and imitate his life of selfless service (8:35-37). For the success of their work, Jesus' ministers need prayer (9:29), restful retreat (6:31), and confidence that the Lord is working through them (11:22-24).

Working in Jesus' name, the disciples can expect persecution and possibly martyrdom (13:13), but if people welcome them, they in turn will be assured of their reward (9:41).

Ministers need to be courageous. Ministry is a public witnessing (4:21-25) to a "faithless and corrupt age" (8:38). Although suffering and persecution will result (13:9-13), the minister must persevere in the prophetic calling (8:38; 13:13).

Mark's community sees itself as an extension of Jesus' preaching, teaching, and exorcizing ministry. Mark firmly reminds them that successful Church ministry requires above all companionship with Jesus (3:13, 20, 32; 4:10, 36; 6:31; 7:17; 8:10, 27; 9:30-31, 33; 10:32; 13:1; 14:7). Called to ministry, the Church trains Christ's followers to live in union with the Lord and in fellowship with other disciples. The Church proclaims the kingdom to a crisis-filled world, calling all to live in anticipation of the Lord's final return. Jesus' own life of selfless service is the only authentic model for the Church.

Conclusion
SPIRITUALITY FOR A TIME OF UNCERTAINTY

Mark is one of the most significant prophetical figures in the early Church. Others before him had challenged the injustices of society, and the immorality of individuals, and called all alike to deepen their faith in Jesus as Lord. Mark does all this, but he also calls his community to read the signs of the times, identify the problems, and prepare themselves, personally and institutionally, for the conflicts and sufferings ahead. He challenges his community to reassess the foundations of their spiritual life and redefine the authentic message of Jesus. He is the first Christian writer to launch a major challenge to the institutional Church, critically assessing its structures, attitudes, and teachings. He is one of the most daring figures of the early Church, challenging his community to return to the true sources of their faith and reject the secondary accretions of history, to reject the comfort zone of religion and face the need to suffer for Christ's sake, to reaffirm Christ's gift of freedom from law, institutions, and pressures of the powerful. Although Mark's is referred to as "the sorrowful gospel," it is also a joyful liberation.

Mark is an evangelist of courageous determination, who sifts early religious traditions and gives direction to the nascent Church. He is the first theologian of early Christianity to bring order into the many oral traditions about Jesus. Unwilling to cling to nonessentials, he is vigorously opposed to accommodating the message to socially acceptable forms of religion; his no-frills gospel forces believers to focus their faith on essentials.

Mark is an exciting proclaimer of the gospel, his work an enduring masterpiece. The envy of preachers, his account of the message of Jesus affects the reader or listener by drawing each one to participation, response, and dedication. The vigor and vitality of his gospel generates more enthusiasm and faith than any other writing of early Christianity.

Mark is a visionary. Seeing the end of the apostolic generation and anticipating the worldwide dissemination of the message of Jesus, he preserves for future generations the first consecutive presentation of the ministry and teachings of Jesus. His account, showing little interest in chronology, has a perennial dimension to it. In Mark's finished work, Jesus is ministering to us now, wherever we are.

Mark is the spiritual theologian of Christian suffering. He centers his story on Jesus' journey to the cross, recalls to disciples of all times the centrality of Christian suffering, and spiritually prepares his own community for the suffering and persecution he knows they must anticipate. His passion story is scripture's most moving account of the Lord's sufferings. The dying Jesus, rejected by all, arouses remorse, pain, and sorrow in disciples of every age. Although he focuses on suffering and excludes a developed theology of resurrection, Mark still retains a spirit of hope, confidence, and encouragement.

Mark is a servant leader who calls other leaders to conversion in their Christian leadership styles. He denounces the clinging to power, the pursuit of status, the desire to monopolize and control followers, and the yearning for privileges. His portrait of Christ, the servant leader, presents him as a model of effective ministry and liberating leadership. His condemnation of abuses of authority by the Pharisees, scribes, disciples, and relatives of Jesus are warnings to all who serve others in the Church.

Mark gives us a multidimensional portrait of Jesus. His simple and dramatic christology, unencumbered by later embellishments, gives us a realistic presentation of how disciples saw and understood Jesus. Jesus is so human in Mark that all can identify with him. Immersed in humanity's strengths and limitations, the Markan Jesus is alive, real, and humanly challenging. He is also a great teacher whose words of power are confirmed by mighty deeds. But the human and suffering Jesus, who dies abandoned by the world, is the beloved Son of God, and the agent of final judgement. Mark calls each believer to integrate faith in both the man of suffering and the Son of God.

Mark presents both the strengths and weaknesses of the great disciples of Jesus, thereby encouraging all believers in their weaknesses and warning them in their moments of strength that others, far greater than they, have failed and betrayed the Lord, but been converted in the end. Mark calls for vigilance in all the disciples of Jesus so that their dedication will not waver under the threats that all must face, individually and institutionally.

Mark reminds us that Jesus inaugurated the reign of God, and Mark calls his community to establish their own place in it. This new period in history requires new institutional responses. The community's repentance, faith, mutual service, sharing, and outreach in service are their way of establishing the reign of God. Mark calls his community to distinguish between God's will for them and human traditions, to maintain simple structures, and value leadership in faith. The kingdom will be maintained in spite of each generation's crises, as the members live as pilgrims awaiting the end, witnessing to the Lord through the trials and persecutions of each period of history. They minister in Jesus' name, reaching out to all nations, as they proclaim the times of fulfillment.

Christian churches today face the double problem of fidelity and relevance. The authenticity of ecclesiastical structures and doctrinal formulations are questioned regarding their fidelity to sources and their relevance for today. This constant and deep questioning provokes divisions between the churches and polarization within each community. At times this painful experience produces bitterness and persecution. In the late eighties and early nineties much of the suffering of Christians will come from fellow believers as the conflict and crises over doctrinal formulations and ecclesiastical structures continue. Mark's gospel. written in times of uncertainty, becomes a powerful and appropriate summons to Christians today. His prophetical challenge, courageous call to focus on essentials, visionary insight into missionary relevance, and emphasis on a spirituality of suffering and mutual service highlight the essentials of responsible Christian living in the next decade. His portrait of Jesus, the kingdom, communal mission, and discipleship are simple and radical, encouraging and full of warning, exciting and appealing.

In previous centuries, Mark was igorned or modified to make his message more acceptable. The churches today need to face up to his rigorous challenge.

NOTES

INTRODUCTION

[1]Henry Wansbrough, "St. Mark," *A New Catholic Commentary on Holy Scripture* (London: Nelson, 1969), p. 955.

[2]David Rhoads and Donald Michie, *Mark as Story* (Philadelphia: Fortress Press, 1983), p. xi.

[3]Sean P. Kealy, "Mark: Hope for Our Tragic Times," *Biblical Theology Bulletin*, 12 (1982), pp. 128-130.

[4]See John F. O'Grady, *Mark: the Sorrowful Gospel* (New York: Paulist Press, 1981).

CHAPTER ONE

[1]Papias is quoted by Eusebius in his *Church History*, iii. 39. 15: "And the Elder said this also: Mark, having become the interpreter of Peter, wrote down accurately all that he remembered of the things said and done by the Lord, but not in order. For neither did he hear the Lord, nor did he follow Him, but afterwards, as I said, Peter. . .adapted his teachings to the needs (of the hearers), but not as though he were drawing up a connected account of the Lord's oracles. So then Mark made no mistake in thus recording some things just as he remembered them, for he made it his one care to omit nothing that he had heard and to make no false statement therein."

[2]Justin the martyr, writing around 161, quotes Mark 3:17 in his *Dialogue*, 106, and refers to it as "Peter's memoirs." Irenaeus, in his *Adversus Haereses*, iii. I. 2, says "And after the death of these Mark, the disciple and interpreter of Peter, also transmitted to us in writing the things preached by Peter." Clement of Alexandria is twice quoted by Eusebius in his *Church History*, vi. 14. 6, and ii. 15. 2, and also writes in his own *Adumbr. in I Pet. v. 13:* "Mark, the follower of Peter, while Peter was preaching publicly the gospel at Rome in the presence of certain of Caesar's knights and was putting forward many testimonies concerning Christ, being requested by them that they might be able to commit to memory the things which were being spoken, wrote from the things which were spoken by Peter, the Gospel which is called according to

Mark." In *Church History*, iv. 25. 5, Eusebius also quotes Origen: "And second, that according to Mark, who did as Peter instructed him, whom also he acknowledged as a son in the Catholic Epistle in these words, 'She that is in Babylon, elect together with you, saluteth you, and Mark my son.'" Tertullian, writing against Marcion (iv. 5), says "And what Mark published may be said to be Peter's whose interpreter Mark was." Jerome, in his commentary on Matthew (Prooemium, 6) writes: "Second, Mark, the interpreter of the apostle Peter and the first Bishop of the Church of Alexandria, who himself did not see the Lord the Saviour, but narrated those things which he heard his master preaching, with fidelity to the deeds rather than to their order."

[3]The Anti-marcionite prologue states: "Mark. . .who is called 'stump-fingered,' because he had rather small fingers in comparison with the stature of the rest of his body. . .was the interpreter of Peter. After the death of Peter himself he wrote down this same gospel in the regions of Italy." The Muratorian Canon adds: "At some things he was present, and so he recorded them."

[4]C. E. B. Cranfield, "Gospel of Mark," *The Interpreter's Dictionary of the Bible*, vol. 3 (New York: Abingdon Press, 1962), p. 268; *The Gospel According to Saint Mark* (Cambridge: University Press, 1972), p. 5; Vincent Taylor, *The Gospel According to St. Mark* (London: Macmillan Publishing Co., 1966), p. 26; John Bowman, *The Gospel of Mark* (Leiden: E. J. Brill, 1965), p. 22.

[5]See Pierson Parker, "The Authorship of the Second Gospel," *Perspectives in Religious Studies*, 5 (1978), p. 5.

[6]Rhoads and Michie, p. xii.

[7]See Parker, "Authorship," pp. 4-9.

[8]See Cranfield, "Gospel of Mark," p. 272: "There is very little, if anything, that can justifiably he claimed as distinctively Pauline."

[9]St. Augustine, *De Consensu Evangelistarum*, I, 2; also Sherman E. Johnson, *The Gospel According to St Mark* (London: Adam and Charles Black, 1972), p. 16.

[10]Mark actually omits the principal episodes concerning Peter as recorded in the other evangelists: Mt 16:17-19; Lk 22:31-32; Jn 21:15-18.

[11]Wansbrough, "St. Mark," p. 954.

[12]See Henry Barclay Swete, *The Gospel According to St. Mark* (New York: MacMillan Publishing Co., 1908), p. cxiv.

[13]See R. H. Lightfoot, *The Gospel Message of St. Mark*, (Oxford: Clarendon Press, 1950), pp. 2-3.

[14]See Howard Clark Kee, *Community of the New Age: Studies in Mark's Gospel* (Philadelphia: The Westminster Press, 1977), p. 16.

[15]For more extensive treatment of the sources used by Matthew, see Leonard Doohan, *Matthew: Spirituality for the 80s and 90s* (Santa Fe: Bear and Co., 1985), pp. 13-17; for Luke's sources see *Luke: The Perennial Spirituality* (Santa Fe: Bear and Co., 1985), pp. 25-36; and for the

detailed developments of biblical criticism, see *Luke*, pp. 155-172.

[16]See William R. Farmer, *The Synoptic Problem* (New York: MacMillan Publishing Co., 1964); "Modern Developments of Griesbach's Hypothesis," *New Testament Studies*, 23 (1976-77), pp. 275-295; *New Synoptic Studies* (Macon, Georgia: Mercer University Press, 1983); G. Murray, "The Order in St Mark's Gospel," *Downside Review*, 101 (1983), pp. 182-186.

[17]See J. C. O'Neill, "The Synoptic Problem," *New Testament Studies*, 21 (1974-75), pp. 273-285; P. Rolland, "Marc, première harmonie évangelique?" *Revue Biblique*, 90 (1983), pp. 23-79.

[18]See Johnson, p. 28.

[19]See Johnson, p. 26.

[20]William L. Lane, *The Gospel According to Mark* (Grand Rapids, Michigan: William B. Eerdmans Publishing Co., 1974), p. 11; K. Romaniuk, "Le Problème des Paulinismes dans l'Evangile de Marc," *New Testament Studies*, 23 (1976-77), pp. 266-274; Taylor, *Mark*, pp. 127-129.

[21]See Cranfield, *Mark*, p. 11.

[22]See Taylor, p. 77.

[23]See Paul J. Achtemeier, "Toward The Isolation of Pre-Markan Miracle Catenae," *Journal of Biblical Literature* 89 (1970), pp. 265-291; "The Origin and Function of the Pre-Marcan Miracle Catenae," *Journal of Biblical Literature*, 91 (1972), pp. 198-221.

[24]See Norman Perrin and Dennis C. Duling, *The New Testament: An Introduction*, 2nd ed. (New York: Harcourt Brace and Jovanovich, Inc., 1982), p. 235.

[25]See Perrin and Duling, p. 234.

[26]See Perrin and Duling, p. 234.

[27]See Kee, *Community of the New Age*, p. 32.

[28]See Kee, p. 30.

[29]See Vassiliadis Petros, "Behind Mark: Towards a Written Source," *New Testament Studies*, 20 (1973-74), pp. 155-160. Petros suggests the following sections make up the source: 4:24b; 12:38b; 13:5b, 9f, 33f; and possibly 13:15b.

[30]W. G. Kümmel, *Introduction to the New Testament* (London: SCM Press Ltd., 1965), p. 63.

[31]For a synthesis of issues relating to the sources, see Taylor, pp. 67-77; Kümmel, pp. 63-68.

[32]See Taylor, pp. 78-79.

[33]See Joachim Jeremias, *The Parables of Jesus* (London: SCM Press Ltd., 1972), p. 11.

[34]The parables are The Sower (Mk 4:3-8); The seed that grows by itself (Mk 4:26-29); The Mustard Seed (Mk 4:30-32); The Wicked Husbandmen (Mk 12:1-11); The Budding Fig Tree (13:28-31); The Doorkeeper (13:33-37).

[35]See Etienne Trocmé, who identifies the following: wisdom sayings

4:21-25; 8:35-37; prophetic and apocalyptic sayings 13:5-27, 30-37; legal sayings 7:14-23; 9:35-50, *The Formation of the Gospel According to Mark* (Philadelphia: The Westminster Press, 1975), pp. 37-38

[36]See Kee, who lists the following controversies: 2:1-10, 13-17, 18-20, 23-28; 3:1-6, 22, 28-30; 7:1-23; 8:11-13; 10:1-12, 17-31; 11:27-33; 12:13-17, 18-27, 28-34, 35-37a, 37b-40, *Community of the New Age*, p. 38.

[37]See Achtemeier, "Toward The Isolation of Pre-Marcan Miracle Catenae," pp. 265-291.

[38]See Taylor, p. 53.

[39]See Taylor, pp. 82-85.

[40]Wansbrough, p. 955; Trocmé, p. 72.

[41]See Beda Rigaux, *The Testimony of St. Mark* (Chicago: Franciscan Herald Press, 1966), p. 126.

[42]See *Time*, March 10, 1980, p. 65.

[43]Rigaux, p. 61.

[44]Lane, p. 26.

[45]Lane, p. 26.

[46]Taylor, p. 112.

[47]See Kee, *Community of the New Age*, p. 47.

[48]See Rhoads and Michie, p. 47.

[49]See A. Stock, "Chiastic Awareness and Education in Antiquity," *Biblical Theology Bulletin*, 14 (1984), pp. 23-27.

[50]See Augustine Stock, *Call to Discipleship* (Wilmington, Delaware: Michael Glazier, Inc., 1982), pp. 40-53.

[51]See Rhoads and Michie, pp. 38-39; James I. Resseguie, "Reader-Response Criticism and the Synoptic Gospels," *Journal of The American Academy of Religion*, 52 (1984), pp. 307-324.

[52]See Sean P. Kealy, *Mark's Gospel: A History of Its Interpretation* (New York: Paulist Press, 1982), p. 28.

[53]See Jack Dean Kingsbury, "The Gospel of Mark in Current Research," *Religious Studies Review*, 5 (1979), p. 101; L. E. Keck, "The Introduction to Mark's Gospel," *New Testament Studies*, 12 (1965-66), p. 352.

[54]Willi Marxsen, *Mark the Evangelist* (New York: Abingdon Press, 1969), pp. 204-205; see also p. 132.

[55]For a criticism of Marxsen's position, see Lane, *Mark*, p. 6.

[56]For surveys of recent Markan studies, see Howard Clark Kee, "Mark as Redactor and Theologian: A Survey of Some Recent Markan Studies," *Journal of Biblical Literature*, 90 (1971), pp. 333-336; Norman Perrin, "The Interpretation of the Gospel of Mark," *Interpretation*, 30 (1976), pp. 115-124; D. Senior, "The Gospel of Mark," *Bible Today*, 17 (1979), pp. 2096-2104; H. M. Humphrey, *A Bibliography for the Gospel of Mark, 1954-80* (New York: Edwin Mellen Press, 1981); B. G. Powley, "Revisiting Mark," *Scripture Bulletin*, 12 (1981), pp. 40-45; Daniel J. Harrington, "A Map of Books on Mark," *Biblical Theology Bulletin*, 15 (1985), pp. 12-16.

[57]For a detailed summary of the work of these authors, see Kealy, *Mark's Gospel: A History*, pp. 159-197.

[58]Perrin, "Interpretation," p. 120.

[59]Donald Senior, "The Eucharist in Mark: Mission, Reconciliation, Hope," *Biblical Theology Bulletin*, 12 (1982), p. 67.

[60]Perrin, "Interpretation," p. 124.

[61]See D. L. Bartlett, "Biblical Scholarship Today: A Diversity of New Approaches," *Christian Century*, 98 (1981), pp. 1090-94; G. T. Montague, "The Process of Interpreting the Bible," *Bible Today*, 20 (1982), pp. 38-44.

[62]Kealy, *Mark's Gospel: A History*, p. 223.

[63]Rhoads and Michie, p. 4.

[64]For other works of literary criticism, see D. Harrington, "Map," p. 13.

[65]Resseguie, p. 308.

CHAPTER TWO

[1]See Hosea 11:1; Jeremiah 2:1-37; Psalms 68, 78, 95, 106; John L. McKenzie, "Desert," *Dictionary of the Bible*, (Bruce Publishing Co., 1965), pp. 194-196; Xavier León-Dufour, "Desert," *Dictionary of Biblical Theology* (London: Geoffrey Chapman Ltd., 1967), pp. 98-101.

[2]See Mark 1:3, 35-39, 45; 6:31-32, 45-46; 9:2.

[3]Lane, *Mark*, p. 225, says: "Jesus' directive to withdraw to a wilderness-place signifies more than a deserved rest after strenuous labor. What is in view is the concept of rest within the wilderness."

[4]Ulrich W. Mauser, *Christ in the Wilderness* (Naperville, Illinois: A. R. Allenson, 1963), p. 58.

[5]See McKenzie, pp. 781-782.

[6]See E. S. Malbon, "The Jesus of Mark and the Sea of Galilee," *Journal of Biblical Literature*, 103 (1984), pp. 363-377.

[7]See Marxsen, p. 108; for opposing views, see W. D. Davies, *The Gospel and the Land* (Los Angeles: University of California Press, 1974), p. 222.

[8]See A. de Q. Robin, "The Cursing of the Fig Tree in Mark XI. A Hypothesis," *New Testament Studies*, 8 (1961-62), pp. 276-281; also Davies, p. 338.

[9]See A. M. Ambrozic, *The Hidden Kingdom*, The Catholic Biblical Quarterly Monograph Series, vol. 2 (Washington, D. C., CBA., 1972), p. 41.

[10]See T. A. Burkill, *New Light on the Earliest Gospel* (Ithaca, N.Y.: Cornell University Press, 1972), p. 108.

[11]See James M. Robinson, *A New Quest of the Historical Jesus* (London: SCM Press Ltd., 1959), p. 35.

[12]Regarding criteria for distinguishing the authentic words of Jesus from the interpretations or comments of the early communities or evangelists, see Duling and Perrin, pp. 281, 288-289; Norman Perrin,

What is Redaction Criticism? (Philadelphia: Fortress Press, 1969), p. 71; Edgar V. McKnight, *What is Form Criticism?* (Philadelphia: Fortress Press, 1969), pp. 66, 77-78. These authors suggest the following criteria: distinctiveness or dissimilarity—preaching that is clearly different from ancient Judaism; multiple attestation—themes referred to frequently in a cross-section view of the writings; consistency or coherence—teaching that is in keeping with other teaching considered authentic (this one acts as compensation to the criteria of dissimilarity); linguistic and environmental tests—does the context of the material fit into the environment of the day or not.

[13]See E. Schweizer, "Mark's Contribution to the Quest of the Historical Jesus," *New Testament Studies*, 10 (1963-64), pp. 421-432.

[14]Burkill, *Mysterious Revelation*, p. 1; "St. Mark's Philosophy of History," *New Testament Studies*, 3 (1956-57), pp. 142-48.

[15]See McKnight, pp. 62-63, where he summarizes the opinions of Bultmann and Perrin, who distinguish between historical knowledge or the factual information about Jesus, historic knowledge or the historical which is significant to us in our own day, and faith-knowledge or the knowledge which includes acknowledgement of Jesus as Lord.

[16]Robinson, *Quest*, p. 80.

[17]See Stock, *Call to Discipleship*, p. 44.

[18]Lane, pp. 444-445.

[19]James M. Robinson, *The Problem of History in Mark* (London: SCM Press Ltd., 1957), p. 52.

[20]Lane, p. 300.

CHAPTER THREE

[1]Kee, *Community of the New Age*, p. 1.

[2]P. J. Achtemeier, *Mark* (Philadelphia: Fortress Press, 1975), p. 50.

[3]For a synthesis of these positions see Hugh Anderson, *The Gospel of Mark* (London: Oliphants, 1976), pp. 34-35.

[4]Jan Lambrecht, "The Christology of Mark," *Biblical Theology Bulletin*, 3 (1973), p. 272.

[5]Theodore J. Weeden, "The Cross as Power in Weakness," *The Passion in Mark*, Werner H. Kelber, ed. (Philadelphia: Fortress Press, 1976), p. 133.

[6]Trocmé, p. 196.

[7]John R. Donahue, "From Passion Tradition to Passion Narrative," *The Passion in Mark*, Werner H. Kelber ed., pp. 11-12.

[8]Wilfrid Harrington, *Mark* (Wilmington, DEL: Michael Glazier, Inc., 1979), p. 58.

[9]See Augustine Stock, "Hinge Transitions in Mark's Gospel," *Biblical Theology Bulletin*, 15 (1985), pp. 27-31. The conclusions of this article

are included in the outline I propose.

[10]See Lane, *Mark*, p. 141.

[11]Trocmé, p. 99.

[12]Kee, *Community of the New Age*, p. 41.

[13]Rhoads and Michie, p. 120.

[14]Werner H. Kelber, *The Kingdom in Mark* (Philadelphia: Fortress Press, 1974), p. 101.

[15]See Marxsen, p. 66; Theodore J. Weeden, *Traditions in Conflict* (Philadelphia: Fortress Press, 1971), p. 112; Kelber, *Kingdom*, p. 107; Kee, *Community of the New Age*, p. 8, who gives other authors of the same position. For reaction to the idea of tension between Galilee and Jerusalem, see Burkhill, *Mysterious Revelation*, pp. 252-257.

[16]Werner H. Kelber, *Mark's Story of Jesus* (Philadelphia: Fortress Press, 1979), p. 94.

[17]Weeden, *Traditions in Conflict*, pp. 50-51, concludes "Mark is assiduously involved in a vendetta against the disciples. He is intent on totally discrediting them. He paints them as obtuse, obdurate, recalcitrant men who at first are unperceptive to Jesus' messiahship, then oppose its style and character, and finally totally reject it. As a coup de grace, Mark closes his Gospel without rehabilitating the disciples." For a rejection of Weeden's polemical interpretation, see D. Senior, "The Gospel of Mark," p. 2102.

[18]See Rhoads and Michie, p. 128.

[19]Trocmé concludes: "We are accordingly entitled to conclude that the author of Mark is not a very enthusiastic defender of the rights of Simon Peter and even occasionally gives an inkling of his reservations regarding a leader of the Church whose great authority he nevertheless accepts." For an opposing position see Ernest Best, "The Role of the Disciples in Mark," *New Testament Studies* 23 (1976-77), p. 383: "If we take all this together we see that wherever there were references to Peter in the tradition which showed him in a bad light Mark has weakened them in some way or other, and where Mark has introduced Peter into the tradition he has done so either to show him as a spokesman who acts as a foil to Jesus in drawing out his teaching or to show the probability of his repentance from his denial and of his ultimate acceptance by Christ after the resurrection."

[20]See Ernst Lohmeyer, *Galiläa und Jerusalem* (Göttingen: Vandenhoek and Ruprecht, 1936); R. H. Lightfoot, *Locality and Doctrine in the Gospels* (New York: Harper and Row, 1938); Marxsen, *Mark*; Pierson Parker, "Mark, Acts and Galilean Christianity," *New Testament Studies*, 16 (1969-70), pp. 295-304.

[21]Kee, *Community of the New Age*, p. 176.

[22]See Trocmé, p. 259; against Palestine as a location, see Johnson p. 15.

[23]See Anti-marcionite Prologue and Clement of Alexandria in chapter one; 1 Peter 5:13 refers to Mark being in Rome; Mk 15:21 mentions

Rufus as Simon of Cyrene's son, possibly the same as mentioned in Rm 16:13. One problem with Rome as the place of origin is Clement of Rome's seeming ignorance of the gospel.

[24]4:21; 5:9, 15; 6:27, 37; 7:4; 12:14, 42; 15:5, 16, 39, 44-45. Against the value of the Latinisms for supporting a Roman origin, Johnson, p. 16, says: "His Latinisms cannot be used as an argument for the Roman origin of the gospel, since Latin words were used in Greek—even in Hebrew—in various parts of the Empire."

[25]Against Rome, Kee, *Community of the New Age*, p. 102, comments: "Although the traditional locale, Rome, is chronologically possible, the preservation in Mark of cultural and linguistic features of the Eastern Mediterranean rural or village culture—features which Luke, in writing for a Gentile audience, eliminates or alters—speaks against Rome."

[26]Kelber, *Kingdom*, p. 1, is an example of an author who supports a date after the fall; as does S. G. F. Brandon, "The Date of the Markan Gospel," *New Testament Studies*, 7 (1960-61), pp. 126-141.

[27]See E. E. Ellis, "Dating the New Testament," *New Testament Studies*, 26 (1979-80), pp. 487-502.

CHAPTER FOUR

[1]See *Luke: The Perennial Spirituality*, pp. 67-86.

[2]1:1, 24; 3:11; 5:7; 14:61; 15:39, see also 15:34. See Harry L. Chronis, "The Torn Veil: Cultus and Christology in Mark 15:37-39," *Journal of Biblical Literature*, 101 (1982), p. 105, where he affirms that Son of God is only used of Jesus by the Father and the spirit-world prior to the revelation at the cross.

[3]4:26, 30; 9:1, 47; 10:14, 15, 23; 12:34; 15:43.

[4]Burkill, *Mysterious Revelation*, p. 69.

[5]William Wrede, *The Messianic Secret* (London: James Clark and Co. Ltd., 1971), p. 67; see also J. C. O'Neill, "The Silence of Jesus," *New Testament Studies*, 15 (1968-69), pp. 153-167; S. Brown, "Secret of the Kingdom of God," *Journal of Biblical Literature*, 92 (1973), p. 63.

[6]See the various theories in G. H. Boobyer, "The Secrecy Motif in St Mark's Gospel," *New Testament Studies*, 6 (1959-60), pp. 225-235.

[7]Taylor, p. 123.

[8]Kee, *Community of the New Age*, p. 96.

[9]See Kee, p. 173.

[10]Schweizer, "Mark's Contribution to the Quest of the Historical Jesus," p. 431.

[11]Robert A. Spivey and D. Moody Smith, *Anatomy of the New Testament*, 3rd ed. (New York: MacMillan Publishing Co., 1982), p. 94.

[12]John J. Kilgallen, "The Messianic Secret and Mark's Purpose," *Biblical Theology Bulletin*, 7 (1977), pp. 60-65.

[13]Lane, pp. 364-365.

[14]John Dominic Crossan, *Cliffs of Fall: Paradox and Polyvalence in the Parables of Jesus* (New York: The Seabury Press, 1980), pp. 16-17.

[15]Achtemeier, *Mark*, p. 60.

[16]1:21, 22; 2:13; 4:1, 2; 6:2, 30, 34; 7:7; 8:31; 9:31; 10:1; 11:17; 12:14, 35; 14:49. The four that are not editorial are 6:30; 7:7; 12:14; 14:49.

[17]See also Paul J. Achtemeier, " 'He Taught Them Many Things': Reflections on Marcan Christology," *Catholic Biblical Quarterly*, 42 (1980), pp. 465-481.

[18]Achtemier, *Mark*, p. 61, says "Even more interesting is the fact that of the 31 instances where Mark uses one of the three words meaning specifically 'teacher' or 'teaching,' there are only five of those which both Matthew and Luke have decided to reproduce, and in twenty of those cases, neither Matthew nor Luke chose to reproduce it. Either they drop the material, or substitute other vocabulary. Whatever else that may mean, it tends to indicate that Mark used this kind of language in a way that, in the majority of cases, neither Matthew nor Luke felt was particularly appropriate."

[19]Lane, p. 144.

[20]Robinson, *The Problem of History*, p. 50.

[21]The five miracles of nature are 4:35-41; 6:30-44, 45-52; 8:1-10; 11:12-14; the four exorcisms 1:21-28; 5:1-20; 7:31-37; 9:14-29; the eight healings 1:29-31, 40-45; 2:1-12; 3:1-6; 5:25-34; 7:24-30; 8:22-26; 10:46-52; the raising from the dead 5:21-24 and 35-43; the three summaries of Jesus' healings are 1:32-34; 3:7-12; 6:53-56; and the summary on the significance of exorcism 3.20-30.

[22]Achtemeier, "He Taught," p. 479.

[23]Stock, *Call to Discipleship*, p. 147.

[24]Burkill, p. 62.

[25]See Anderson, p. 37, where he lists the following references to verbs of motion: 1:9, 14, 21, 24, 29, 35, 38; 2:1, 13; 3:1; 8:31; 9:30; 10:32.

[26]See J. F. O'Grady, "The Passion in Mark," *Biblical Theology Bulletin*, 10 (1980), pp. 83-87; Georg Strecker, "The Passion and Resurrection Predictions in Mark's Gospel (Mark 8:31; 9:31; 10:32-34)," *Interpretation*, 22 (1968), pp. 421-442.

[27]See Weeden, "The Cross as Power in Weakness," p. 115.

[28]See Rhoads and Michie, p. 87.

[29]See David Stanley, "Mark's Passion-Narrative. Four proleptic symbolic acts (10:46-11:25)," *Way (Supplement)*, 46 (1983), pp. 67-77.

[30]Donald Senior, *The Passion of Jesus in the Gospel of Mark* (Wilmington, Delaware: Michael Glazier, Inc., 1984), p. 15.

[31]See Senior, *Passion*, pp. 9-11, where he gives the spectrum of opinions regarding whether Mark's passion account is dependent on a pre-existing narrative or is a Markan construction.

[32]See Achtemeier, *Mark*, p. 89; Werner H. Kelber, "From Passion

Narrative to Gospel," *The Passion in Mark*, pp. 156-157.

[33]See Senior, *Passion*, p. 51: "The account of the preparation will repeatedly refer to the Passover (14:12 (*x 2*), 14, 16) clearly indicating that Mark understands the meal that follows as a Passover meal (even though the description of the meal itself does not necessarily identify it as a Passover celebration)." Burkill, *Mysterious Revelation*, p. 259, states: "But if Jesus was arrested before the feast began, the last supper could not have been a paschal meal; he was already dead when the passover was eaten." For a good explanation of the development of the Church's understanding of the Last Supper from Mark's primitive form, see Burkill, pp. 258-279.

[34]Kelber, *Mark's Story of Jesus*, p. 75.

[35]See R. S. Barbour, "Gethsemane in the Tradition of the Passion," *New Testament Studies*, 16 (1969-1970), pp. 231-251.

[36]For a list of specific discrepancies, see Senior, *Passion*, p. 88; John R. Donahue, "Temple, Trial and Royal Christology," *The Passion in Mark*, Werner H. Kelber, ed., p. 61.

[37]See Donahue, "Temple, Trial and Royal Christology," p. 62.

[38]Donahue, "From Passion Tradition to Passion Narrative," pp. 6-7.

[39]See Achtemeier, *Mark*, p. 83; also Trocme, p. 60.

[40]Senior, *Passion*, p. 139; see O'Neill, "Silence," pp. 163-164.

[41]Senior, *Passion*, p. 125.

[42]Donahue, "From Passion Tradition," gives the following parallels between Mark and the Psalms: 14:18 = Ps 41:9; 14:34 = Ps 42:6, 11; 43:5; 15:23 = Ps 69:21; 15:24 = Ps 22:18; 15:29 = Ps 22:7; 109:25; 15:36 = Ps 69:21; in "Temple, Trial and Royal Christology," he parallels Jesus' and David's suffering: 14:26, 33 = 2 Samuel 15:30; 14:33 = 2 Sam 15:19-24; 14:29 = 2 Sam 15:19-21; 14:47 = 2 Sam 16:9-11; 14:27 = Zechariah 13:7; 14:42 = 2 Sam 15:31. Regarding Jesus and the Just One, see Ps 27:12; 31:4; 35:4, 11; 38:12, 14-16; 39:9; 55:14-21; 71:10; 109:2.

[43]John R. Donahue, "A Neglected Factor in the Theology of Mark," *Journal of Biblical Literature*, 101 (1982), p. 573, lists the following reactions of amazement to Jesus: "(1). . .conclusion to miracles, 1:27; 2:12; 4:41; 5:15, 20, 33, 42; 6:50, 51; 7:37; (2) in reaction to teaching, 1:22; 6:2; 10:24, 26; 11:18; 12:17; (3) in narratives of divine epiphanies, 4:41; 6:50-51; 9:6; 16:5; (4) over predictions of suffering, 9:32; 10:32, cf. 14:33; (5) of opponents, 11:18; 12:12; 15:5, 44."

[44]Rhoads and Michie, p. 103.

[45]See Lane, pp. 236-237.

[46]See Howard Clark Kee, *Understanding The New Testament*, 4th ed., (Englewood Cliffs, New Jersey: Prentice Hall, Inc., 1983), p. 102: "Some interpreters have suggested a link between the voice and the rabbinic notion that God would attest the right interpretation of the Law of Moses by a celestial echo, bath qol (meaning 'daughter of the voice'), since Jewish piety assumed that the voice of God itself could not be directly heard by humans."

[47]See E. Nardoni, "A Redactional Interpretation of Mk 9,1," *Catholic Biblical Quarterly,* 43 (1981), p. 383. Kelber, *Kingdom,* points out that 324 verses precede the transfiguration scene and 335 follow it. See also J. A. McGuckin, "Jesus Transfigured: A Question of Christology," *Clergy Review,* 69 (1984), pp. 271-279; for parallels between the Old Testament and the transfiguration, see Lane, p. 320.

[48]See Morna Hooker, *Son of Man in Mark* (London: SPCK, 1967), p. 29; also R. H. Fuller, *The Foundations of New Testament Christology* (New York: Scribner's, 1965), p. 42.

[49]Norman Perrin, "The High Priest's Question and Jesus' Answer," *The Passion in Mark,* Werner H. Kelber, ed., p. 90; C. Tuckett, "The Present Son of Man," *Journal of the Study of the New Testament,* 14 (1982), pp. 58-81.

[50]Hooker, p. 179.

CHAPTER FIVE

[1]Schweizer, *Mark*, p. 386.

[2]A. Wilkie, "Discipleship in Mark," *Bible Today,* 11 (1973), p. 1249.

[3]See J. V. Zeitz, "Stages of Faith and the Gospel of Mark," *Spirituality Today,* 36 (1984), pp. 322-332; F. J. Moloney, "Vocation of the Disciples in the Gospel of Mark," *Salesianum,* 43 (1981), pp. 487-516.

[4]Rhoads and Michie, p. 123.

[5]See Donald Senior, "The Eucharist in Mark," pp. 67-68.

[6]David J. Hawkin, "The Incomprehension of the Disciples in the Marcan Redaction," *Journal of Biblical Literature,* 91 (1972), p. 500.

[7]See Lane, pp. 410-411.

[8]See G. Biguzzi, "Mc. 11, 23-25 e il Pater," *Rivista Biblica,* 27 (1979), pp. 57-68.

[9]Vernon K. Robbins, "Last Meal: Preparation, Betrayal, and Absence," *The Passion in Mark,* Werner H. Kelber, ed., p. 29.

[10]See Harry Fleddermann, "The Discipleship Discourse (Mark 9:33-50)," *Catholic Biblical Quarterly,* 1981), p. 57; also Lane, pp. 338-339.

[11]See Daniel Malone, "Riches and Discipleship: Mark 10:23-31," *Biblical Theology Bulletin,* 9 (1979), p. 83.

[12]See R. A. Culpepper, "Mark 10:50: Why Mention the Garment?" *Journal of Biblical Literature,* 101 (1982), pp. 131-132; M. G. Steinhauser, "Part of a 'Call Story'?" *Expository Times,* 94 (1983), pp. 204-206.

[13]Lane, p. 365.

[14]See Lane, p. 367-369.

[15]See Ernest Best, *Following Jesus,* (Journal of the Studies of the New Testament, Supplement Series, 4, Sheffield, 1981), p. 101.

[16]See R. N. Brown, "Jesus and the Child as a Model of Spirituality," *Irish Biblical Studies,* 4 (1982), pp. 178-192.

[17]Rhoads and Michie, p. 126.

[18]Kelber, *Mark's Story of Jesus*, p. 71.

[19]See Harry Fleddermann, "The Flight of a Naked Young Man (Mark 14:51-52)," *Catholic Biblical Quarterly*, 41 (1979), pp. 412-418; Werner H. Kelber, "The Hour of the Son of Man and the Temptation of the Disciples," *The Passion in Mark*, W. Kelber, ed., p. 57: "With Gethsemane Mk has made it unmistakably clear that it was over the issue of suffering Messiahship that Jesus and his disciples parted in conflict."

[20]Senior, *Passion*, p. 37.

[21]Best, "The Role of the Disciples in Mark," p. 401.

[22]See Doohan, *Luke*, pp. 99-100; *Matthew*, pp. 113-117.

[23]Best, *Following Jesus*, p. 204.

[24]Elizabeth Struthers Malbon, "Fallible Followers: Women and Men in the Gospel of Mark," *Semeia*, 28 (1983), p. 31.

[25]Best, *Following Jesus*, p. 63.

[26]Rhoads and Michie, pp. 129-130.

[27]See M. J. Schierling, "Women as Leaders in the Marcan Communities," *Listening*, 15 (1980), pp. 250-256.

[28]See W. Munro, "Women Disciples in Mark?" *Catholic Biblical Quarterly*, 44 (1982), pp. 225-241.

[29]See J. J. Schmitt, "Women in Mark's Gospel," *Bible Today*, 19 (1981), pp. 228-233.

[30]See Malbon, p. 33.

[31]See Malbon, p. 37; Kelber, *Kingdom*, p. 61.

[32]Malbon, p. 40.

[33]Malbon, p. 32.

CHAPTER SIX

[1]John R. Donahue, "Jesus as the Parable of God in the Gospel of Mark," *Interpretation*, 32 (1978), p. 378.

[2]See Norman Perrin, *Jesus and the Language of the Kingdom* (Philadelphia: Fortress Press, 1976), p. 33.

[3]Kelber, *Kingdom*, p. 42.

[4]See Burkill, *Mysterious Revelations*, p. 18.

[5]See Lane, p. 452.

[6]Dorothey M. Slusser and Gerald H. Slusser, *The Jesus of Mark's Gospel* (Philadelphia: The Westminster Press, 1952), p. 69.

[7]See Crossan, p. 26.

[8]Crossan, p. 49, says: "It is not just a parable of the Kingdom, although it is that as well, but rather a metaparable, it is a parable about parables of the Kingdom."

[9]See Kelber, *Mark's Story of Jesus*, p. 15.

[10]See Lane, p. 165.

[11] Lane, p. 166.

[12] Lane, p. 168.

[13] Trocme, p. 162, gives the following references to house: 1:29; 2:1, 15 (?); 3:20; 7:17, 24; 9:28, 33; 10:10; see also Best, *Following Jesus*, p. 231.

[14] See Best, *Following Jesus*, p. 231.

[15] Kee, *Community of the New Age*, p. 110.

[16] See Kee, "Mark's Portrayal of his Community," *Community of the New Age*, pp. 107-116.

[17] See William L. Countryman, "How Many Baskets Full? Mark 8:14-21 and The Value of Miracles in Mark," *Catholic Biblical Quarterly*, 47 (1985), p. 648.

[18] See Lane, p. 269.

[19] See H. W. Montefiore, "Revolt in the Desert," *New Testament Studies*, 8 (1962), pp. 135-141.

[20] Robbins, "Last Meal," p. 34.

[21] See J. R. Donahue, *The Theology and Setting of Discipleship in the Gospel of Mark* (Milwaukee, WI: Marquette University Press, 1983).

[22] Kelber, *Mark's Story of Jesus*, p. 89.

[23] See Trocme, p. 214.

[24] See Mark 3:14; 4:10; 6:7; 9:35; 10:32; 11:11; 14:10, 17, 20, 43.

[25] See Weeden, *Traditions*, p. 42.

[26] See E. Best, "Peter in the Gospel according to Mark," *Catholic Biblical Quarterly*, 40 (1978), pp. 547-558.

[27] Weeden, *Traditions*, p. 98.

[28] See Kee, *Community of the New Age*, pp. 44-45.

[29] Kelber, *Kingdom*, p. 109.

[30] Stock, *Call to Discipleship*, pp. 171-172.

[31] See Ambrozic, p. 42.

[32] See Kelber, *Kingdom*, p. 134. For an excellent review of the characteristics of apocalyptic literature and their relationship to Mark, see Kee, *Community of the New Age*, pp. 64-76.

[33] Kee, p. 145.

[34] Lane, p. 133.

[35] See Kathleen M. Fisher and Urban C. von Wahlde, "The Miracles of Mark 4:35-5:43: Their Meaning and Function in the Gospel Framework," *Biblical Theology Bulletin*, 11 (1981), pp. 13-16; also J. D. M. Derrett, "Peace, Sandals and Shirts (Mark 6:6b-13 par.)," *Heythrop Journal*, 24 (1983), pp. 253-265.

[36] Thomas E. Boomershine, "Mark 16:8 and the Apostolic Commission," *Journal of Biblical Literature*, 100 (1981), p. 237.

[37] Kelber, *Mark's Story of Jesus*, p. 42.

[38] Kelber, *Kingdom*, p. 61.

[39] Perrin and Duling, p. 243.

[40] See M. F. Kirby, "Mark's Prerequisite for Being an Apostle," *Bible Today*, 18, (1980), pp. 77-81.

152

[41]See Helen Doohan, "Ministry in Mark," *Scripture in Church*, 15 (1985), pp. 343-350.

Bibliography

Achtemeier, Paul J. "Toward The Isolation of Pre-Marcan Miracle Catenae." *Journal of Biblical Literature*, 89 (1970), pp. 265-291.
--- "The Origin and Function of the Pre-Marcan Miracle Catenae." *Journal of Biblical Literature*, 91 (1972), pp. 198-221.
--- *Mark*. Philadelphia: Fortress Press, 1975.
--- " 'He Taught Them Many Things': Reflections on Marcan Christology." *Catholic Biblical Quarterly*, 42 (1980), pp. 465-481.
Ambrozic, A. M. *The Hidden Kingdom*. The Catholic Biblical Quarterly Monograph Series, vol. 2. Washington, D. C.: CBA, 1972.
Anderson, Hugh. *The Gospel of Mark*. London: Oliphants, 1976.
Barbour, R. S. "Gethsemane in the Tradition of the Passion." *New Testament Studies*, 16 (1969-70), pp. 231-251.
Bartlett, D. L. "Biblical Scholarship Today: A Diversity of New Approaches." *Christian Century*, 98 (1981), pp. 1090-1094.
Best, Ernest. "The Role of the Disciples in Mark." *New Testament Studies*, 23 (1976-77), pp. 377-401.
--- Peter in the Gospel according to Mark." *Catholic Biblical Quarterly*, 40 1978), pp. 547-558.
--- *Following Jesus*. Journal of the Studies of the New Testament Supplement Series, 4, Sheffield, 1981.
Biguzzi, G. "Mc. 11, 23-25 e il Pater." *Rivista Biblica*, 27 1979) pp. 57-68.
Boobyer, G. H. "The Secrecy Motif in St. Mark's Gospel." *New Testament Studies*, 6 (1959-1960), pp. 225-235.
Boomershine, Thomas E. "Mark 16:8 and the Apostolic Commission." *Journal of Biblical Literature*, 100 (1981), pp. 225-239.
Bowman, John. *The Gospel of Mark*. Leiden: E. J. Brill, 1965.
Brandon, S. G. F. "The Date of the Markan Gospel." *New Testament Studies*, 7 (1960-61), pp. 126-141.
Brown, R. N. "Jesus and the Child as a Model of Spirituality." *Irish Biblical Studies*, 4 (1982), pp. 178-192.
Brown, S. "Secret of the Kingdom of God." *Journal of Biblical Literature*, 92 (1973), pp. 60-74.
Burkill, T. A. "St. Mark's Philosophy of History." *New Testament Studies*, 3 (1956-57), pp. 142-148.
--- *Mysterious Revelation*. Itacha, N. Y.: Cornell University Press, 1963.
--- *New Light on the Earliest Gospel*. Ithaca, N. Y.: Cornell University Press, 1972.
Chronis, Harry L. "The Torn Veil: Cultus and Christology in Mark 15:37-39." *Journal of Biblical Literature*, 101 (1982), pp. 94-114.

Countryman, William L. "How Many Baskets Full? Mark 8:14-21 and The Value of Miracles in Mark." *Catholic Biblical Quarterly*, 47 (1985), pp. 643-655.

Cranfield, C. E. B. "Gospel of Mark." *The Interpreter's Dictionary of the Bible*. New York: Abingdom Press, 1962, vol. 3. pp. 267-277.

--- *The Gospel According to Saint Mark*. Cambridge: University Press, 1972.

Crossan, John Dominic. *Cliffs of Fall: Paradox and Polyvalence in the Parables of Jesus*. New York: The Seabury Press, 1980.

Culpepper, R. A. "Mark 10:50: Why Mention the Garment?"*Journal of Biblical Literature*, 101 (1982), pp. 131-132.

Davies, W. D. *The Gospel and the Land*. Los Angeles: University of Califonia Press, 1974.

Derrett, J. D. M. "Peace, Sandals and Shirts (Mark 6:6b-13 par.)." *Heythrop Journal*, 24 (1983), pp. 253-265.

Donahue, John R. "From Passion Tradition to Passion Narrative." *The Passion in Mark*. Werner H. Kelber, ed., pp. 1-20.

--- "Temple, Trial and Royal Christology." *The Passion in Mark*. Werner H. Kelber, ed., pp. 61-79.

--- "Jesus as the Parable of God in the Gospel of Mark." *Interpretation*, 32 (1978), pp. 369-386.

--- "A Neglected Factor in the Theology of Mark." *Journal of Biblical Literature*, 101 (1982), pp. 563-594.

--- *The Theology and Setting of Discipleship in the Gospel of Mark*." Milwaukee, Wisconsin: Marquette University Press, 1983.

Doohan, Helen. "Ministry in Mark." *Scripture in Church*, 15 (1985), pp. 343-350.

Doohan, Leonard. *Luke: The Perennial Spirituality*. 2nd ed. Santa Fe: Bear and Co., 1985.

--- *Matthew: Spirituality for the 80s and 90s*. Santa Fe: Bear and Co., 1985.

Ellis, E. E. "Dating the New Testament." *New Testament Studies*, 26 1979-80), pp. 487-502.

Farmer, William R. *The Synoptic Problem*. New York: MacMillan Publishing Co., 1964.

--- "Modern Developments of Griesbach's Hypothesis." *New Testament Studies*, 23 (1976-77), pp. 275-295.

--- *New Synoptic Studies*. Macon: Georgia University Press, 1983.

Fisher, Kathleen M., and Urban C. von Wahlde. "The Miracles of Mark 4:35-5:43: Their Meaning and Function in the Gospel Framework." *Biblical Theology Bulletin*, 11 (1981), pp. 13-16.

Fleddermann, Harry. "The Flight of a Naked Young Man (Mark 14:51-52)." *Catholic Biblical Quarterly*, 41 (1979), pp. 412-418.

--- "The Discipleship Discourse (Mark 9:33-50)." *Catholic Biblical Quarterly*, 43 (1981), pp. 57-75.

Fuller, R. H. *The Foundations of New Testament Christology*. New York: Scribner's, 1965.

154

Harrington, Daniel. "A Map of Books on Mark." *Biblical Theology Bulletin*, 15 (1985), pp. 12-16.

Harrington, Wilfrid. *Mark*. Wilmington, Delaware: Michael Glazier, Inc., 1979.

Hawkin, David J. "The Incomprehension of the Disciples in the Marcan Redaction." *Journal of Biblical Literature*, 91 (1972), pp. 491-500.

Hooker, Morna. *Son of Man in Mark*. London: SPCK, 1967.

Humphrey, H. M. *A Bibliography for the Gospel of Mark, 1954-80*. New York: Edwin Mellen Press, 1981.

Jeremias, Joachim. *The Parables of Jesus*. London: SCM Press Ltd., 1972.

Johnson, Sherman E. *The Gospel According to St. Mark*. London: Adam and Charles Black, 1972.

Kealy, Sean P. "Mark: Hope for Our Tragic Times." *Biblical Theology Bulletin*, 12 (1982), pp. 128-130.

--- *Mark's Gospel: A History of Its Interpretation*. New York: Paulist Press, 1982.

Keck, L. E. "The Introduction to Mark's Gospel." *New Testament Studies*, 12 (1965-66), pp. 352-370.

Kee, Howard Clark. "Mark as Redactor and Theologian: A Survey of some Recent Marcan Studies." *Journal of Biblical Literature*, 90 (1971), pp. 333-336.

--- *Community of the New Age: Studies in Mark's Gospel*. Philadelphia: The Westminster Press, 1977.

--- *Understanding the New Testament*, 4th ed. Englewood Cliffs, New Jersey: Prentice Hall, Inc., 1983.

Kelber, Werner H. *The Kingdom in Mark*. Philadelphia: Fortress Press, 1974.

--- *Mark's Story of Jesus*. Philadelphia: Fortress Press, 1979.

--- "The Hour of the Son of Man and the Temptation of the Disciples." *The Passion in Mark*. W. Kelber, ed., pp. 41-60.

--- ed. *The Passion in Mark*. Philadelphia: Fortress Press, 1976.

Kilgallen, John J. "The Messianic Secret and Mark's Purpose." *Biblical Theology Bulletin*, 7 (1977), pp. 60-65.

Kingsbury, Jack Dean. "The Gospel of Mark in Current Research." *Religious Studies Review*, 5 (1979), pp.. 101-107.

Kirby, M. F. "Mark's Prerequisite for Being an Apostle." *Bible Today*, 18 (1980), pp. 77-81.

Kummel, W. G. *Introduction to the New Testament*. London: SCM Press, Ltd., 1965.

Lambrecht, Jan. "The Christology of Mark." *Biblical Theology Bulletin*, 3 (1973), pp. 256-273.

Lane, William L. *The Gospel According to Mark*. Grand Rapids, Michigan: William B. Eerdmans Publishing Co., 1974.

Leon-Dufour, Xavier. "Desert." *Dictionary of Biblical Theology*. London: Geoffrey Chapman, Ltd., 1967, pp. 98-101.

Lightfoot, R. H. *Locality and Doctrine in the Gospels*. New York: Harper and Row, 1938.

--- *The Gospel Message of Mark*. Oxford: Clarendon Press, 1950.

Lohmeyer, Ernst. *Galilaa und Jerusalem*. Gottingen: Vandenhoek and Ruprecht, 1936.

Malbon, Elizabeth Struthers. "Fallible Followers: Women and Men in the Gospel of Mark." *Semeia*, 28 (1983), pp. 29-48.

--- "The Jesus of Mark and the Sea of Galilaa." *Journal of Biblical Literature*, 103 (1984), pp. 363-377.

Malone, Daniel. "Riches and Discipleship: Mark 10:23-31." *Biblical Theology Bulletin*, 9 (1979), pp. 78-88.

Marxsen, Willi. *Mark the Evangelist*. New York: Abingdon Press, 1969.

Mauser, Ulrich W. *Christ in the Wilderness*. Naperville, Illinois: A. R. Allenson, 1963.

McGuckin, J. A. "Jesus Transfigured: A Question of Christology." *Clergy Review*, 69 (1984), pp. 271-279.

McKenzie, John L. "Desert." *Dictionary of the Bible*, New York: Bruce Publishing Co., 1965, pp. 194-196.

McKnight, Edgar V. *What is Form Criticism?* Philadelphia: Fortress Press, 1969.

Moloney, Francis J. "Vocation of the Disciples in the Gospel of Mark." *Salesianum*, 43 (1981), pp. 487-516.

Montague, G. T. "The Process of Interpreting the Bible." *Bible Today*, 20 (1982), pp. 38-44.

Montefiore, H. W. "Revolt in the Desert." *New Testament Studies*, 8 (1962), pp. 135-141.

Munro, W. "Women Disciples in Mark?" *Catholic Biblical Quarterly*, 44 (1982), pp. 225-241.

Murray, G. "The Order in St Mark's Gospel." *Downside Review*, 101 (1983), pp. 182-186.

Nardoni, E. "A Redactional Interpretation of Mark 9,1." *Catholic Biblical Quarterly*, 43 (1981), pp. 365-384.

O'Grady, John F. "The Passion in Mark." *Biblical Theology Bulletin*, 10 (1980), pp. 83-87.

--- *Mark: The Sorrowful Gospel*. New York: Paulist Press, 1981.

O'Neill, J. C. "The Silence of Jesus." *New Testament Studies*, 15 (1968-69), pp. 153-167.

--- "The Synoptic Problem." *New Testament Studies*, 21 (1974-75), pp. 273-285.

Parker, Pierson. "Mark, Acts and Galilean Christianity." *New Testament Studies*, 16 (1969-70), pp. 295-304.

--- "The Authorship of the Second Gospel." *Perspectives in Religious Studies*, 5 (1978), pp. 4-9.

Perrin, Norman. *What is Redaction Criticism?* Philadelphia: Fortress Press, 1969.

--- *Jesus and the Language of the Kingdom*. Philadelphia: Fortress Press, 1976.

--- "The Interpretation of the Gospel of Mark." *Interpretation*, 30 (1976), pp. 115-124.

--- "The High Priest's Question and Jesus' Answer." *The Passion in Mark*, Werner H. Kelber, ed., pp. 80-95.

Perrin, Norman, and Duling, Dennis C. *The New Testament: An Introduction*, 2nd ed. New York: Harcourt Brace and Jovanovich, Inc., 1982.

Petros, Vassiliadis. "Behind Mark: Towards a Written Source." *New Testament Studies*, 20 (1973-74), pp. 155-160.

Powley, B. G. "Revisiting Mark." *Scripture Bulletin*, 12 (1981), pp. 40-45.

Resseguie, James I. "Reader-Response Criticism and the Synoptic Gospels." *Journal of The American Academy of Religion*, 52 (1984), pp. 307-324.

Rhoads, David, and Michie, Donald. *Mark as Story*. Philadelphia: Fortress Press, 1982.

Rigaux, Beda. *The Testimony of St. Mark*. Chicago: Franciscan Herald Press, 1966.

Robbins, Vernon, K. "Last Meal: Preparation, Betrayal and Absence." *The Passion in Mark*. Werner H. Kelber, ed., pp. 21-40.

Robin, A. de Q. "The Cursing of the Fig Tree in Mark XI. A Hypothesis." *New Testament Studies*, 8 (1961-62), pp. 276-281.

Robinson, J. M. *The Problem of History in Mark*. London: SCM Press Ltd., 1957.

---*A New Quest of the Historical Jesus*. London: SCM Press Ltd., 1959.

Rolland, P. "Marc, premiére harmonie évangelique?" Revue Biblique, 90 (1983), pp. 23-79.

Romaniuk, K. "Problème des Paulinismes dans l'Evangile de Marc." *New Testament Studies*, 23 (1976-77), pp. 266-274.

Schlierling, M. J. "Women as Leaders in the Marcan Communities." *Listening*, 15 (1980), pp. 250-256.

Schmitt, J. J. "Women in Mark's Gospel." *Bible Today*, 19 (1981), pp. 228-233.

Schweizer, E. "Mark's Contribution to the Quest of the Historical Jesus." *New Testament Studies*, 10 (1963-64), pp. 421-432.

--- *The Good News According to Mark*. Atlanta: John Knox Press, 1976.

Senior, Donald. "The Gospel of Mark." *Bible Today*, 17 (1979), pp. 2096-2104.

--- "The Eucharist in Mark: Mission, Reconciliation, Hope." *Biblical Theology Bulletin*, 12 (1982), pp. 67-72.

--- *The Passion of Jesus in the Gospel of Mark*. Wilmington, Delaware: Michael Glazier, Inc., 1984.

Slusser, Dorothy M., and Gerald H. Slusser. *The Jesus of Mark's Gospel*. Philadelphia: The Westminster Press, 1952.

Spivey, Robert A. and Smith, D. Moody. *Anatomy of the New Testament*, 3rd. ed. New York: MacMillan Publishing Co., 1982.

Steinhauser, M. G. "Part of a 'Call Story'?" *Expository Times*, 94 (1983), pp. 204-206.

Stock, Augustine. *Call to Discipleship*. Wilmington, Delaware: Michael Glazier, Inc., 1982.

--- "Chiastic Awareness and Education in Antiquity." *Biblical Theology Bulletin*, 14 (1984), pp. 23-27.

--- "Hinge Transitions in Mark's Gospel." *Biblical Theology Bulletin*, 15 (1985), pp. 27-31.

Strecker, Georg. "The Passion and Resurrection Predictions in Mark's Gospel (Mark 8:31; 9:31; 10:32-34)." *Interpretation*, 22 (1968), pp. 421-442.

Swete, Henry Barclay. *The Gospel According to St. Mark*. New York: MacMillan Publishing Co., 1908.

Taylor, Vincent. *The Gospel According to St. Mark*. London: MacMillan Publishing Co., 1966.

Trocmé, Etienne. *The Formation of the Gospel According to Mark*. Philadelphia: The Westminster Press, 1975.

Tuckett, C. "The Present Son of Man." *Journal of the Study of the New Testament*, 14 (1982), pp. 58-81.

Wansbrough, Henry. "S. Mark." *A New Catholic Commentary of Holy Scripture*. London: Nelson, 1969.

Weeden, Theodore J. *Traditions in Conflict*. Philadelphia: Fortress Press, 1971.

--- "The Cross as Power in Weakness." *The Passion in Mark*. Werner H. Kelber, ed., pp. 115-134.

Wilkie, A. "Discipleship in Mark." *Bible Today*, 11 (1973), pp. 1249-1251.

Wrede, William. *The Messianic Secret*. London: James Clark and Co., Ltd., 1971.

Zeitz, J. V. "Stages of Faith and the Gospel of Mark." *Spirituality Today*, 36 (1984), pp. 322-332.

Index of Subjects

Index of Authors

Index of Scriptural References

NOTES

NOTES